THE LURE OF ESTHER MOUNTAIN
MATRIARCH OF THE ADIRONDACK HIGH PEAKS

THE LURE OF ESTHER MOUNTAIN

MATRIARCH OF THE ADIRONDACK HIGH PEAKS

BY SANDRA WEBER

PURPLE MOUNTAIN PRESS

FLEISCHMANNS, NEW YORK

Permission to reprint the following is gratefully acknowledged:

"Esther" (song) by Sandra Weber and Peggy Eyres, copyright 1994 by Peggy Eyres/BMI.

Penny Wiktorek, "Legends of the Adirondacks" in *Of the Summits, of the Forests*, ed. Tim Tefft (Morrisville, NY: Adirondack Forty-Sixers, 1991), 233-5. Courtesy of the Adirondack Forty-Sixers.

From the Russell Carson Papers, Adirondack Museum Library. Courtesy of the Adirondack Museum, Blue Mountain Lake, New York.

"Life Story of James M. Wolfe, Civil War Veteran," (1931), 1. Courtesy of Doug Wolfe.

First edition
1995

Published by Purple Mountain Press, Ltd.
Main Street, P.O. Box E3
Fleischmanns, New York 12430-0378

Copyright © 1995 by Sandra Weber

All rights reserved under International and
Pan-American Copyright Conventions.

Library of Congress Cataloging-in-Publication Data

Weber, Sandra, 1961-
    The lure of Esther Mountain : matriarch of the Adirondack high peaks / by Sandra Weber. -- 1st ed.
    Includes bibliographical references.
    ISBN 0-935796-65-7 (pbk. : alk. paper)
    1. Esther Mountain (N.Y.)--History. 2. Natural history--New York (State)--Esther Mountain. I. Title.
F127.A2W37   1995
974.7'53--dc20   95-4724
                                                                                                               CIP

Original etchings by Ryland Loos:
Front cover and frontispiece: "Esther Climbing Esther."
Back cover: "Esther—Whiteface's Lady of the North."

Manufactured in the United States of America.
Printed on acid-free paper.

ESTHER
by Sandra Weber and Peggy Eyres

Esther grew up close to Whiteface Mountain,
Thought she heard it calling her name.
Her family told her, "Ladies don't go climbing."
Esther thought she'd try it just the same.

One morning just before the dawn was breaking,
Esther loaded up her brother's pack.
She left behind her petticoats and ribbons;
Esther wouldn't let them hold her back.

(Chorus)
Sometimes you have to climb a mountain.
Sometimes you have to wade a stream.
When the path you follow disappears among the trees,
Be brave and follow your dream.

By mid-morning she was tired and hungry.
Still she climbed beside a rocky creek.
By evening she fell down amid the hobble bush,
Not far from another mountains peak.

Her family found her early the next morning,
Shivering cold but glad to be alive.
They named the peak she conquered, Esther Mountain,
For the young girl who was lost but still survived.

(Chorus)

If you dare to set out on a mountain,
And find you've somehow gone astray,
Though you miss your final destination,
Look at what you've learned along the way.

You took one step then followed with another,
Found the inner courage to go on.
You reached new heights and felt your heart's direction.
Now you finally see yourself as strong.

(Chorus)

© 1994 by Peggy Eyres /BMI

TABLE OF CONTENTS

Esther Song	5
Acknowledgments	8
Why Esther?	9
Birthmarks	11
Early Settlers	17
Esther Combs--First Climber	25
Russell French--First Trail Blazer	29
J. & J. Rogers Company--Landowners and Loggers	38
Russell Carson--First Historian	45
Grace Hudowalski--First Steward	52
New Developments	56
Dr. Edwin H. Ketchledge--Educator	62
A Guided Tour	68
Conclusion	73
Notes	75

Facing page: View of Whiteface Mountain and highway from the summit of Esther Mountain. Photo by the author.

ACKNOWLEDGMENTS

TWO YEARS AGO, I started down a trail searching for Esther McComb. My guide was Russ Carson. His personal papers at the Adirondack Museum in Blue Mountain Lake led me through the process of his discovery of Esther in 1923. The kindness and foresight of Russ Carson in preserving his letters and stories and making them available to researchers is greatly appreciated. Thanks to the Adirondack Museum and Shirley (Carson) Kendall for permission to include excerpts from Russ Carson's letters in this book.

Grateful acknowledgment is also made to the Adirondack Museum, Saranac Lake Free Library, and Keene Valley Library for permission to print photos from their collections.

I want to acknowledge four individuals who gave immeasurable help: Jerold Pepper, librarian at the Adirondack Museum, was a valuable source of materials and advice; Ed Ketchledge generously offered his insight and guidance and warmly shared his view of Esther; Grace Hudowalski provided her personal notes, photos, and unending spirit to the project; and Jim Goodwin's letters always brightened my day and made the stories come to life!

Thanks to the many others who provided input, especially Doug Wolfe, Don Peterson, Ryland Loos, Peggy Eyres, Nancie Battaglia, Jim Swedberg, Jim Meehan, Bruce Cole, Janet Decker, Harold Schwalenstocker, Steve Golasa, Erika and Sal Carrara, Ed and Alice Stanley, the Adirondack Forty-Sixers, and the MCCC Writers Club.

Thanks to my family and friends for their encouragement. Ron, thanks for being such a pain and an inspiration. Thanks to my in-laws for those quality weekends they spent with their grandchildren. And a special thank you to Diane Weber for her reassuring words and valuable review comments.

My greatest appreciation goes to my husband, Bill, and my daughters, Emily and Marcy, for their support and patience as I searched through cemeteries, libraries, museums, and courthouse basements looking for Esther. Thanks for letting me follow my dream.

WHY ESTHER?

NORTH OF NEW YORK CITY, Albany, and Saratoga Springs lies the boundary of the Adirondack Park. This grand park encompasses Lake Placid, Lake George, Lake Tear-of-the-Clouds, Old Forge, Ticonderoga, and Keene Valley. At the heart of the park stands a great mountain region known as the Adirondack high peaks.

Marcy, Seymour, Phelps, Donaldson, Porter, and Colvin—many prominent, powerful men have lent their names to these peaks. These men were famous statesmen, guides, scholars, and explorers; their mountain peaks are well known and frequently hiked.

Ten miles to the north of the other peaks stand two isolated high peaks, Whiteface and Esther. The towering, noble Whiteface Mountain dominates the landscape, as well as the literature and history, of the northern region. Esther Mountain stands at the end of a three-mile spur that extends northeast from Whiteface. Esther is relatively unknown and rarely explored; thousands of people drive, hike, or ski to the top of Whiteface and view Esther without knowing its identity or legacy.

Much of what has been written about Whiteface applies to Esther, since the two mountains share a ridge and similar history. However, Esther has different topographic features, diverse agricultural and industrial developments, and fascinating heroes and heroines. It has a special identity and a special lure.

Esther is the matriarch of the Adirondacks. Of the forty-six Adirondack mountains over four thousand feet in elevation, Esther is the only one named for a woman, Esther McComb. She is the only woman credited with a first ascent of a high peak. She made her climb at age fifteen, for the "sheer joy of climbing."

Through the 1800s, Esther Mountain provided valuable natural resources for the Goodspeeds' farms, French's sawmill, and J. & J. Rogers Company's iron forges and paper mill. After New York State purchased the mountain in 1921, it was recognized as the northernmost of the forty-six high peaks. Soon, hikers were climbing through the thick, scratchy cripplebrush to reach its trailless summit. By the mid-1900s, the highest road in the state, the largest ski center in the Adirondacks, and the first family theme park in the country, Santa's Workshop, could be found on Esther's slopes.

Since 1961, Esther Mountain has served as a field site for the State University of New York at Albany, a living laboratory for scientists from all over the world, who come to study cloud chemistry, acid rain, red spruce decline, fir waves, and other activities in Esther's forest.

Although not the most frequented or the best known of the Adirondack high peaks, Esther Mountain has lured farmers, lumbermen, skiers, hikers, scientists—and one adventurous young girl—to its slopes. These folk discovered the mountain's special features, developments, and heroes and heroines.

Listen to the voices. Discover the lure of Esther Mountain.

Looking from the north toward Whiteface—a three-mile spur extends to Esther.
Photo by Edwin H. Ketchledge.

BIRTHMARKS

THE BIRTH AND MATURING of Esther Mountain to its present state took many millions of years. From primeval times to 1800 AD, nature created and dramatically shaped this mountain and its surroundings. Only a few traces of the mountain's long birth remain. The rocks and soil, the trees and rivers, tell the story.

For millions of years, the anorthosite rock that now lies exposed on Esther Mountain's summit was buried beneath fifteen miles of the earth's crust. About ten million years ago, the rock pushed up through northern New York State. The Adirondack high peaks, including Esther Mountain, were born.

Long periods of erosion, uplifting, and glaciation followed. In the last two million years, continental glaciers advanced into the Adirondack valleys and melted back at least three times. The ice sheets buried the summit of Esther Mountain and other high peaks.

A dramatic change occurred about 12,000 years ago during the last Ice Age. The ice sheet shrank and Esther Mountain's slopes emerged, surrounded by valley glaciers. As the ice retreated northward, the land was released from the weight of the thick ice and rose several hundred feet. Even today, "as we roam the Adirondacks, the peaks are rising up under our feet faster than they are being eroded, with a net gain in elevation of some millimeters per year," explain geologists Howard and Elizabeth Jaffe.[1]

Esther and Whiteface mountains, at over four thousand feet, rose above the nearby Sentinel and Wilmington ranges. The closest high peaks were ten miles away to the south.

Millions of years of erosion created the rounded shape of most of the Adirondack summits. Their basic shape was then sculpted by the glacier. Esther's rounded summit was left with newly exposed rock. On Whiteface Mountain, ice carved out the upper slopes and left the peak with three sharp, rocky spurs. In *Forest and Crag*, Laura and Guy Waterman describe the pointed ridges still visible today:

> From the south, as usually seen, it [Whiteface Mountain] stands out as a clear, graceful pyramid, the closest thing to Mount Fuji-like symmetry found in the Northeast. But the northern slopes of Whiteface are less regularly shaped, meandering off in a formless array of ridges and humps. On these northern flanks, before they descend to the lower hills that stretch to Canada, there arises one last swell of forested upland that

forms a subsidiary sister peak to the great Whiteface. This 4,270-foot mountain is designated Esther.[2]

During the last retreat of the ice sheets, a great mass of snow accumulated at the head of a small ravine on the east side of Esther. The freeze-thaw-freeze cycle converted the snow at the bottom of the ravine to ice. As new snowfalls added more weight on top, the ice at the bottom was squeezed up and over the edge of the hollow. The scraping ice gradually enlarged the top of the ravine. Eventually the ice melted and left a deep, hollowed-out bowl known as White Brook Cirque.

On the northern ridge above White Brook, the glacier formed a terminal moraine. The nose of the glacier pushed a mass of glacial debris as it advanced southward. When the ice melted, it left a curved ridge of rock fragments and huge boulders, tumbled smooth and round.

On the summit of Esther Mountain, the ice scraped away the vegetation and exposed the bare rock. As the climate warmed, primitive lichen began to cover the rocks. Pioneering mosses grew. Eventually, patches of soil built up. The wind and the birds carried in seeds. Tundra plants, bushes, flowers, and small trees began to take root among the rocks. But weathering and erosion worked at the rocks and soil. Running water carried away the layer of humus, rich with minerals. The few remaining patches of organic soil limited plant growth at the summit.

Downslope, the water deposited the rich mineral soil and rock particles into ravines and bowls. These areas built up fertile soil for plants and trees; while the thin soil in other areas barely covered the bedrock. Fragile trees sank roots into the dirt on the mountain slopes. The thin soil offered little support against high winds, it drained poorly in rainstorms, and it held no deep water reserves in droughts. The young, pioneering forests were likely ravaged again and again by fire and wind and changing climate. Eventually, as the climate stabilized, hardier tree populations persisted and the forest approached a mature state.

Trees on the upper slopes faced an extremely harsh environment. For every thousand-foot climb, the temperature dropped about three degrees Fahrenheit. A perpetual westerly wind hit the mountain. Icy blasts of cold air swept down from the Arctic and struck the first peaks in their path, Esther and Whiteface Mountains. Most days, misty clouds hung over the mountains. "Three ridges which surround the summit (including nearby Esther Mountain) shoot warm air up to Whiteface's summit, where it cools and caps the peak with a cloud. That's why, when the sky is blue everywhere else, a cloud rests on Whiteface."[3]

Opposite:
Aerial view, 1947, showing White Brook Cirque,
Esther Brook, Red Brook, and Ausable River. USGS.

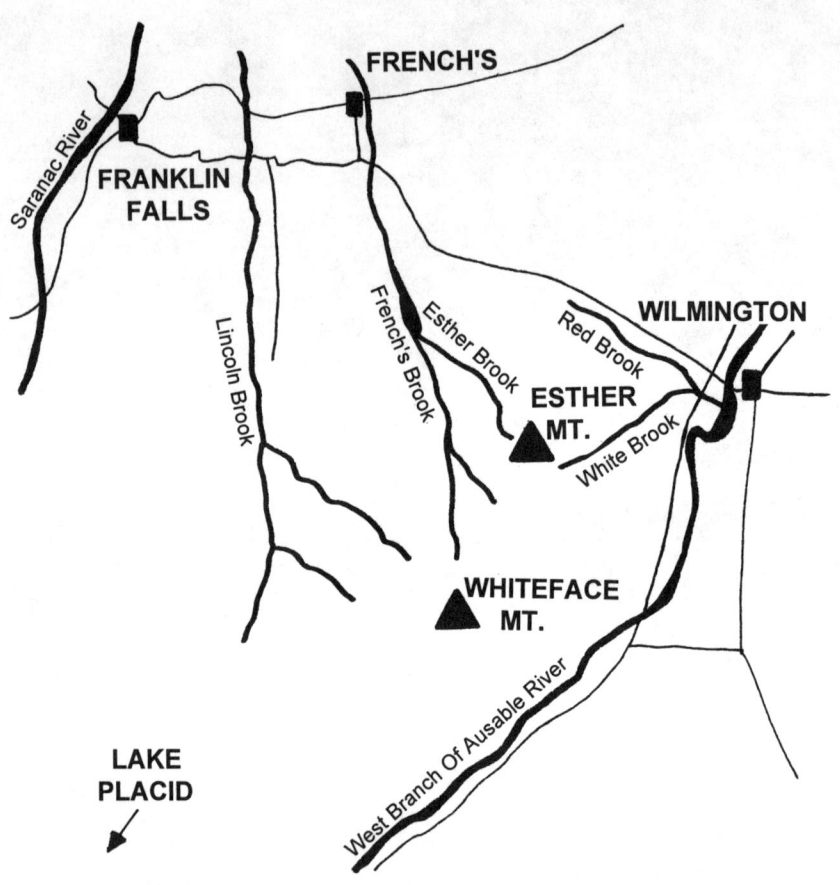

Streams of the Esther Mountain area.
Map by the author.

Most tree species were already at the edge of their northern threshold. They could not survive the cold temperatures, strong winds, and long winters with heavy snowfall. Balsam firs were the only trees growing in those harsh conditions on the open summit, and they grew only a few feet tall. The wind and cold swept over the summit, flattening the tops of the trees, tangling their branches, and turning them into *Krummholz* or *crooked woods*.

Other trees near the mountaintop resembled broomsticks. They managed to push their crowns up above the harsh, icy winds, so that their top branches spread and grew while their trunks remained bare. Other trees looked like flags being whipped by the wind. The wind and ice made it difficult for branches to grow on the side facing the wind. The other side, protected by the trunk, grew normal branches.

Downslope, as temperatures rose and more mineral soil appeared, red spruce mixed with the fir. Red spruce was shade tolerant, long-lived, and well adapted to the colder climate. In drainage basins, such as Esther Brook on the northeast side of the mountain, spruces thrived in the moist, mineral-rich soil that had washed down from the summit. At sites disturbed by fire, wind, or other forces, the vigorous balsam fir took root.

A Natural History of Trees of Eastern and Central North America, by Donald Culross Peattie, explains the folklore regarding this relationship:

> The mountain people recognize the intimate association of the Spruce and Fir by calling them respectively the He-Balsam and the She-Balsam. Observing that the Fir has swollen blisters of resin under the bark, they fancifully compared them to breasts filled with milk; hence the She-Balsam. And supposing perhaps that a mate must be found for the She-Balsam and noting that its companion tree had no resin blisters, they named it the He-Balsam.[4]

The He-Balsam and She-Balsam constituted the mountain forest above 2,500 feet. Little else could survive in the environmentally stressed conditions. On the lower slopes and in the valleys, deep layers of mineral soils existed and a more moderate climate prevailed. Over two dozen tree species grew in these regions, including sugar maple, american beech, yellow birch, eastern hemlock, white pine, oak, and hickory. The abundant hardwoods were harvested for house building, fuel, and timber. The fertile, rich soil was well suited for agricultural use.

The mature forest of the early 1800s held a wealth of other resources: mink, beaver, deer, moose, maple syrup, clean air, and scenic views. However, the forest was dense and hard to penetrate. The accessibility, and the health and diversity, of this rich forest depended on the numerous brooks, streams, and rivers running through it.

Two main rivers paralleled the Esther-Whiteface mountain ridge. Southeast of the ridge was the west branch of the Ausable River flowing northeast through Wilmington and past the foot of Whiteface Mountain. The Ausable plunged 700 feet between the granite cliffs at High Falls Gorge and then slowly meandered through the valley.

The Saranac River, northwest of the ridge, flowed in a northeasterly direction from Saranac Lake through Franklin Falls to Plattsburgh.

Many smaller streams and brooks flowed through the area. Esther Brook and French's Brook flowed down the northwest face of Esther Mountain, through a small pond, and into a large swamp near Forestdale (or French's). Lincoln Brook drained the northwest face of Whiteface Mountain.

White Brook and Red Brook drained the east face of Esther Mountain. At the base of the mountain, they emptied into the west branch of the Ausable River.

Rainwater and snowmelt accumulated in small brooks, like Red Brook, White Brook, and Esther Brook. Great amounts of water flowed from these small brooks and supplied the lowland farm fields, the mighty rivers and canals, and the cities downstate. For many years, population remained downstate and the birthmarks on Esther Mountain remained untouched.

Despite the forces of nature and the hand (and foot) of mankind on the mountain, some of Esther's birthmarks remain today. The rocky summit, the White Brook Cirque, and the rich farm soil along French's Brook remain, as do the broomstick trees, the rounded boulders, the dwarfed balsam firs, and the red spruces along Esther Brook.

Most significant is the birthmark that is not there. There is no slide nor dike nor avalanche on Esther Mountain, so it is often overlooked—overshadowed by gleaming birthmarks on Whiteface Mountain.

Looking from the east toward the sculpted
forms of Whiteface, Lookout, and Esther.
Photo by the author.

EARLY SETTLERS

IT IS DOUBTFUL that more than a few Native Americans ever set foot on Esther Mountain. Some Iroquois and Algonquin ventured into its lowland forests and swamps to hunt deer, moose, and beaver. But, as early white explorers noted, the Iroquois and Algonquins "had no inducement to make the laborious ascent of steril[e] mountain peaks, which they held in superstitious dread, or to explore the hidden sources of the rivers which they send forth... All here seems abandoned to solitude."[1]

By 1790, a few settlers had moved to the valleys and lowland forests. There they found good farming tracts where the land was not too steep or too often flooded. These pioneers had no time or need to explore Esther Mountain; they worked hard at farming and lumbering and attempted to carve out villages. They cleared forests, planted fields, built cabins, and cleared roads.

Most pioneers left or died. A few stubborn survivors stayed and faced the mountain and the forest. In 1798 the town of Jay was formed and named for the governor of New York, John Jay. By 1810, about 180 families lived there, mostly emigrants from Vermont, Massachusetts, and Connecticut. Spafford's *Gazetteer* of 1813 noted, "The inhabitants are laborious, peaceable, good citizens."[2]

Travelers by-passed the mountain on their way north. From Lake Champlain in the east they headed toward St. Regis or the St. Lawrence for fishing and hunting excursions. The few who had the curiosity, courage, or skills to venture into the mountains explored the larger Whiteface Mountain. Surveyors, explorers, and writers were also drawn to Whiteface.

Whiteface Mountain was the first Adirondack peak to be given an English name. It was described in *A Gazetteer of the State of New-York* published in 1813: "The noted cobble, called *Whiteface* mountain, is in this Town [Jay], and overlooks all the country for 100 to 150 miles."[3] Its height was incorrectly reported as 2,600 feet. At the time, the Catskills were thought to be the highest mountains in the state.

Little else was known about this area until 1836, when New York State became interested in valuable ore bodies in the mountains and selected Professor Ebenezer Emmons to survey the area known as the Second Geological District. Professor Emmons, state geologist, and Mr. James Hall, assistant state geologist for the northern region, climbed Whiteface Mountain on September 20, 1836. Using a mountain barometer, they estimated the height to be 4,855 feet, proving that the Adirondacks were the highest mountains in the state.[4]

In his report, Emmons wrote that Whiteface "is about five thousand feet high, and very steep and abrupt upon all sides. It rises immediately from Lake Placid, with a steep slope almost from the eastern border of the lake...standing out by itself from the great cluster of mountains, it overlooks on all sides the surrounding country far and near, and hence is probably the most important one to visit in the whole region." He seemed to foresee the future of Whiteface as a tourist attraction and "as a botanical field, [which] will exceed the other summits for yielding a harvest of alpine plants."[5]

The earliest known photograph of Esther Mountain. The summit of Whiteface Mountain is in the foreground. Photo by Seneca Ray Stoddard, about 1880.
Courtesy of Adirondack Museum, Blue Mountain Lake, NY.

Apparently, Emmons did not see the mountain behind Whiteface, rising over 4,200 feet. No one appears to have noticed it until 1865, when the anonymous author of *The Opening of the Adirondacks* wrote, "In this mountain [Whiteface] is a chasm or gorge, known as the Whiteface Notch; not far from which rises Mount Esther."[6]

While mineral resources attracted the State to the Esther Mountain area, fertile farmland, iron ore, and forests attracted settlers. Three pioneer settlements sprang up near Esther Mountain: the village of Wilmington to the east, the village of Franklin Falls to the northwest, and a family of farmers in the middle. These three settlements cover only ten miles but traverse two counties and three townships.

Whiteface Mountain and Esther Mountain are located in the town of Wilmington, county of Essex. The entire area was part of the town of Jay until 1821, when the town of Danville was formed. On March 22, 1822,

Danville was renamed Wilmington for Wilmington, Vermont, the homeland of the Nye, Hall, and Pierce families.[7]

Colonization of the surrounding valley began with the village of Wilmington, located directly east of Esther Mountain. Every town needed a sawmill; in 1812 Reuben Sanford built one in Wilmington along the Ausable River. By 1822 Sanford had added a gristmill, potash factory, forge, blacksmith shop, inn, church, school, general store, tavern, and two distilleries. His unending energy and initiative attracted other settlers to the Wilmington wilderness.

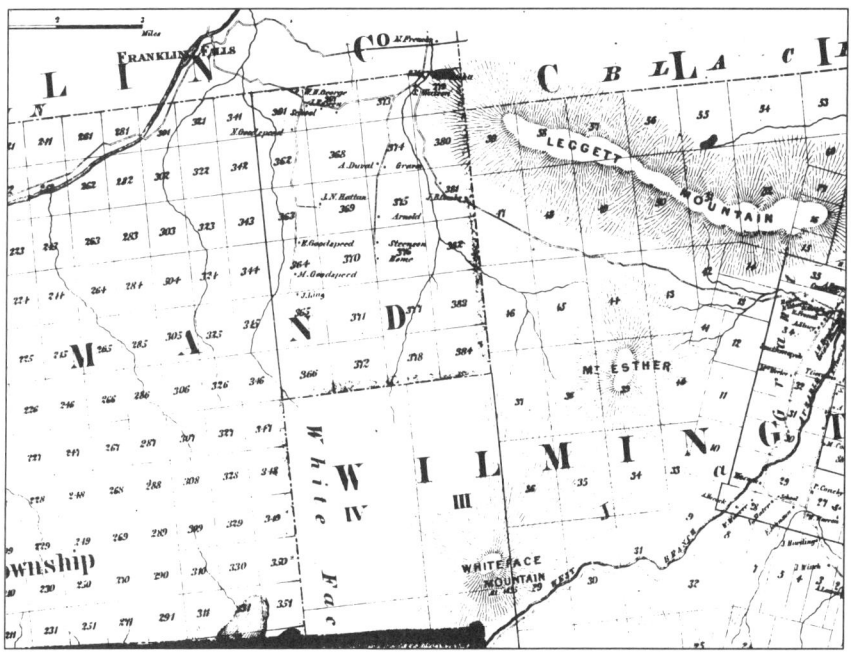

J. H. French map of Essex County, 1858, the first document showing Mt. Esther. The Combs, French, and Goodspeed families are shown in St. Armand.
Courtesy of Adirondack Museum, Blue Mountain Lake, NY.

Reuben Sanford was born in 1780 in Woodbury, Connecticut. He was the seventh of thirteen children of Oliver and Phebe Sanford. Shortly after his birth, the family moved to Poultney, Vermont. Reuben married Polly Lewis on February 16, 1804, and moved to Jay, where Polly bore Paulina, the first of seven daughters. Paulina Sanford was born on September 4, 1805, and died March 12, 1806.

As a major in the War of 1812, Reuben distinguished himself and his fellow Wilmingtonians. At the Battle of Plattsburgh on September 11, 1814, the advance of the British forced the American troops to cross the Saranac River. Major Sanford took an ax and chopped the timbers of the bridge before the British could cross. It is said that one shot from a British gun hit the ax and lodged in the wood Sanford was chopping.[8]

Reuben Sanford served in the New York State Assembly from 1814 to 1817 and was a delegate to the Constitutional Convention in 1821. The first Wilmington town meeting was held at Reuben's house on the first Tuesday of April 1821. In 1828 Reuben became a member of the state Senate. He was also the first postmaster of Wilmington.

At age sixty-nine, Reuben was still farming in Wilmington and owned real estate valued at $5,000. He and Polly lived with Elisha A. and Phebe Adams, their son-in-law and daughter. Another of Sanford's daughters, Eliza, married Amos Avery, the town blacksmith.

By the time of Sanford's death in 1855, the village of Wilmington was a ghost town and seemed destined to remain forgotten. In 1874, guidebook author Seneca Ray Stoddard remarked:

> Wilmington, aside from the hotel, has a deserted, worn-out sort of look, and while it appears to possess a little of every thing it seems as though nothing ever came to a head. Two or three shut-up-looking stores, three shut-up-looking churches—Methodist, Presbyterian and Lutheran—a few scattering houses, an old forge, saw, starch and grist mills, all having a decidedly dead appearance.[9]

In the 1800s, a rough, dirt road led out of Wilmington, up one side of Esther Mountain and down the other. At the bottom of the mountain, the road branched west to Franklin Falls and north to French's. Along the road were many fertile farming tracts with sandy and gravelly soil left by the glacier. French's Brook and Lincoln Brook carried water from Whiteface and Esther Mountains to the farmland. The brooks emptied into the Saranac River and continued east to Lake Champlain.

The history of this area begins with its first pioneers, the Goodspeed family. The Goodspeeds settled the lower slopes of Esther Mountain, formed a new town, and told the story of how Esther Mountain was named.

Nathaniel Goodspeed was the oldest Goodspeed to live in the region. He was the great-great-grandson of Roger Goodspeed, one of the founders of Barnstable, Massachusetts, in 1639. Later, Roger moved his family to Misteake, Massachusetts, where they were probably the first European settlers.[10]

Nathaniel was born June 17, 1749, in Leicester, Massachusetts. He served in the Revolutionary War as a private and is believed to have fought at Bunker Hill. He worked as a blacksmith and was very strong and agile. "Though weighing nearly 300 pounds, he could leap over a string held about five feet from the ground."[11]

Early Settlers/21

Goodspeed Family Tree

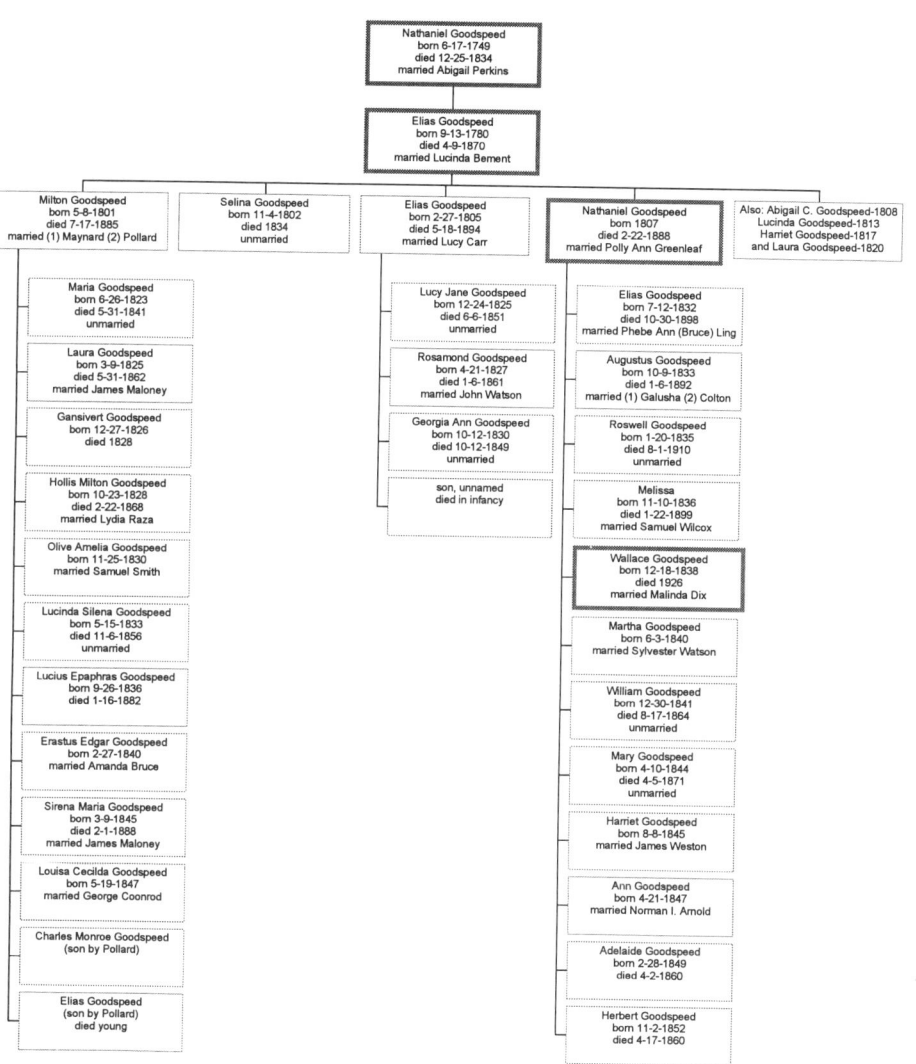

Chart by the author.

Nathaniel and his wife, Abigail Cleveland Perkins, had only one child, Elias. Elias Goodspeed was born in Middlesex, Connecticut, on September 13, 1780. He served as a second lieutenant in the War of 1812. Elias Goodspeed married Lucinda Bement from Massachusetts. They had five daughters and three sons.

About 1829, Elias Goodspeed and two of his sons, Milton and Elias, moved their families from Hawley, Massachusetts, to the banks of Lincoln Brook in Essex County, New York. In 1834 Elias's other son, Nathaniel, moved to Essex County with his wife, Polly, two sons, Elias and Augustus, and grandparents, Nathaniel and Abigail. On Christmas day of 1834, shortly after arriving in Essex County, the elder Nathaniel Goodspeed died. He is buried in the Goodspeed Cemetery beside Lincoln Brook.

On April 23, 1844, the area where the Goodspeeds settled was divided from the town of Wilmington and became the town of St. Armand. The derivation of the name St. Armand is debated. Some believe the town's name comes from the old French name for the Saranac River. Others say it is named after the Canadian town St. Armand, which was the hometown of Charles S. Toof.[12]

St. Armand covers the northwest corner of Essex County. The foothills of Mt. Alton, Pigeon Roost, Owl's Head, Blue Mountain, Shed Hill, and Knapp Hill stand on the west side of Lincoln Brook. The highest mountain in St. Armand is Moose Mountain, which rises 3,699 feet. As shown on the 1858 map, the town boundary line diverts from its straight path to cut out Whiteface and Esther mountains; they remain part of the town of Wilmington.

The first St. Armand town meeting was held at the house of Elias Goodspeed. Goodspeed also served as the first town supervisor in 1844-45. Within a few years, St. Armand had two schools, fifty-four pupils, and two teachers. The town map of 1858 shows one of the schools and the houses of M. Goodspeed, E. Goodspeed, and N. Goodspeed.

In 1855 the Goodspeeds owned 149 improved acres cleared of trees and rocks, and 234 unimproved acres. They grew 49 tons of hay, 95 bushels of spring wheat, 640 bushels of oats, 18 bushels of barley, 78 bushels of buckwheat, 20 bushels of corn, 800 bushels of potatoes, 26 bushels of peas, and 100 bushels of turnips. This seems quite a harvest considering the short summers, low temperatures, and rudimentary tools of the time. This information was recorded by Elias Goodspeed, census taker for the 1855 state census in the town of St. Armand.

Elias led an extraordinary life and was a man of great abilities. Besides holding the positions mentioned earlier, he worked as a teacher, farmer, blacksmith, iron manufacturer and surveyor. He died on April 9, 1870.

Elias's son, Elias, moved to the Lincoln Brook area to farm and make iron. He married Lucy Carr and had four children. By 1840 he had become a minister and moved to the town of Essex.

Elias's other sons, Milton and Nathaniel, put down roots at the base of Esther Mountain. In 1850 Milton Goodspeed was a farmer with $500 property value. He and his wife, Olive Maynard, had ten children. Olive died in 1853. Milton then married Laura Pollard, and they had two sons.

Esther Mountain from Franklin Falls Road. Etching by Ryland Loos.

Nathaniel and his wife, Polly, cleared over 100 acres and built a frame house. They had twelve children: Elias, Augustus, Roswell, Melissa, Wallace, Martha, William, Mary, Harriet, Ann, Hurbert, and Adelaid. "[Nathaniel] spent his life at hard work in the deep woods, reared a large family to lives of usefulness and honor, possessed the respect of all who knew him and finally died of paralysis in 1888, after fifty-four years spent in that locality [St. Armand, N. Y.]."[13]

Nathaniel and Polly's son, Wallace W. Goodspeed, was born on December 18, 1838, in Essex County. Like his father, Wallace became a farmer and led a seemingly quiet life until 1864.

On February 12, 1864, Wallace enlisted in Company D, Regiment 17 of the Vermont Infantry. He signed up at Braintree, Vermont, for a period of three years. In the *Company Descriptive Book*, he is described as "age: 25 years; height: 5 feet 5-3/4 inches; complexion: light; eyes: blue; hair: light; born: St. Armand, NY; occupation: farmer."[14]

Wallace was severely wounded in the head on June 3, 1864, at Cold Harbor. He spent most of July, August, September, and October in hospitals. On August 10, in St. Armand, he married Malinda Dix. By November he was back with his regiment. After the war, Wallace lived and farmed in the Esther Mountain area. In 1875 he was living in a log house near Franklin Falls with his wife and five young daughters.

In 1923, Wallace Goodspeed told the story about Esther McComb and how Esther Mountain was named. He remembered hearing the story when he was a boy. His story was published in 1927 in Russell Carson's book, *Peaks and People of the Adirondacks*. Goodspeed probably never saw the story in print since he died in 1926. He and his wife are buried in the Union Cemetery.

The settlement in St. Armand never became more than a group of scattered farms. By 1880, most of the Goodspeeds had moved from St. Armand. Later, Alfred W. Currier purchased the Goodspeed farm and replaced the farm fields with a plantation of pine trees.

The most significant reminder of the pioneer days is the Goodspeed Cemetery, located on the dirt road beside Lincoln Brook. The tombstone inscriptions reveal the faith, hardship, and love of the Goodspeed family.

ESTHER COMBS—FIRST CLIMBER

THE GOODSPEED FAMILY played an important role in the early history of the Adirondack region: they cleared land, built roads, and started a town. Later, Wallace Goodspeed, grandson of the area's first settler, made a significant contribution by telling the story of how Esther Mountain was named.

Wallace Goodspeed told the story to Charles Beede, a famous Keene Valley guide. Beede passed the story on to Russell Carson, who was writing a book about the forty-six Adirondack high peaks and their name origins, first ascents, and other historical features. In 1927, Wallace Goodspeed's story was retold in Russell Carson's book, *Peaks and People:*

> In 1839, a family by name of McComb lived on this road [between Wilmington and Franklin Falls] at the foot of the mountain. Esther McComb, a fifteen-year-old daughter, had an ambition to climb Whiteface, but her parents were unwilling. Disregarding their wishes, one day Esther started out alone to make the climb. She reached the top of the mountain now bearing her name, but became lost before getting to Whiteface. A searching party was out all night and found her the next morning. Her mother jokingly called the mountain Esther because of the occurrence, but the name was taken up and has remained.[1]

Esther McComb's climb is a most compelling legend. It is the only first ascent of an Adirondack high peak credited to a woman. Esther is the only high peak named for a woman and the first high peak named for an ordinary person who simply enjoyed climbing mountains. Esther McComb's climb was accomplished at a time when the Adirondacks were virtually unexplored; Esther Mountain was only the eighth peak to be ascended.

Over time, the story of Esther's climb was embellished and Esther became a folk heroine to many Adirondack hikers. In *Of the Summits, of the Forests*, Penny Wiktorek writes:

> She was a good girl, obedient and mannerly, traits all parents hope for in a child and train their offspring to be. The McCombs thought they had such a daughter. In all her fifteen years, Esther had never given them reason to believe otherwise, but no human being can ever truly know what is in the mind of another, and the McCombs had no idea what was growing in Esther's mind.

She rose before her parents that morning and stood outside the kitchen door. She looked toward the mountains and toward Whiteface. Oh, to climb that mountain of mountains—bald, no doubt breezy on top, with a view that could fill a soul for a lifetime. If only she could stand on its top just once! It would be enough. She could carry the view from that mountain with her the rest of her life...

Acting without thought and without telling her parents of her plan, she hastened into the kitchen and grabbed a piece of bread and a hunk of cheese...She started forward, determined...

She fought her way through dense brush and thick trees. It was a hard and tiring climb. Eventually, the trail seemed to level off, and she felt relief as by late afternoon, she made her way to a small summit and clearing.

...She nearly staggered as she looked to the southwest. Could that be Whiteface way over there? Then, where was she? How had she missed the turnoff? Her heart sank like lead. She hadn't done it. She hadn't made the summit of Whiteface...

Knowing she could never make it back home tonight, she made herself as comfortable as possible and settled in for the night with a crushing disappointment filling her.

The next morning her father found her. She followed him home, leaving any hope of reaching Whiteface behind.

"No one climbs a mountain unless he's measuring its height or studying it for science," her father spoke angrily. "Mountains are not meant for girls to climb. Don't you ever try such a foolhardy thing again!"

It is believed she didn't, but in the second quarter of the nineteenth century, she had a mountain named after her.[2]

The legend is enchanting but Esther McComb's real life is a mystery. Who was she? Why did she climb the mountain? Is there any written evidence of her life or her climb?

The answers are sketchy; the evidence is intriguing. The J. H. French map of Essex County, printed in 1858, shows "MT. ESTHER" next to "WHITEFACE MOUNTAIN Alt. 4855."[3]

This map is the earliest known published reference to Esther Mountain which indicates that the mountain was named Esther before 1858. Since no altitude is given for Mt. Esther, it probably had not yet been surveyed. (The first evidence of a survey appears only at the end of the century and refers to the peak as "Esther Mountain.") The 1858 map also locates families, schools, cemeteries, sawmills, and churches. No McComb family appears on the map as living near Whiteface Mountain. However, a family named Combs appears at the base of Esther Mountain along the Wilmington-Franklin Falls road. This is exactly where Wallace Goodspeed said Esther McComb lived in 1839.

There may have been confusion among the names McComb, Macomb, and Combs. In a letter dated March 24, 1924, Russell Carson refers to "Esther Combs," not Esther McComb. In a list of mountain names and namesakes, Macomb is circled and Combs is written next to it. In one note, Charles Beede writes the name as "Esther Coombs."[4]

Did Wallace Goodspeed say the family's name was McComb or Combs? Maybe it was both. Back then, people were less precise with names and spellings; they often dropped a prefix like "Mc" or "Mac." The Combs family cited on the map also could have been referred to as the McComb family. Beede's note implies that the common name was Combs, pronounced "kooms," since names were frequently misspelled according to their pronunciation.

Who was the Combs family that lived at the base of Esther Mountain? Thomas Edwards Combs was born on June 29, 1806, in Gill, Massachusetts. He was the third of six children born to Seth and Abigail Combs.[5]

By 1830, Thomas Combs had moved to the town of Lewis, in New York State, where he worked as a farmer and laborer. Thomas married Harriet Lewis, who was born in 1806 in Essex County, New York. Her father was Nathan Lewis, Jr., and his father was Nathan Lewis, one of the first settlers of Elizabethtown in the 1790s.

Census records from 1830 and 1840 show Thomas and Harriet Combs lived in the town of Lewis. They resided in the town of Essex in 1850 and moved to the town of St. Armand in 1855. On April 25, 1855, Thomas E. and Alvah C. Combs of the town of Lewis bought 160 acres and estate property from Charles B. Hatch of the town of Westport. The land was Lot #381 in Military Tract Township 11. The price was $300.[6]

French's Map of 1858 shows "J. B. Combs" on Lot #381 on the Wilmington-Franklin Falls Road (sometimes called the St. Armand Road) just across the eastern boundary of the town of St. Armand. There, at the base of Esther Mountain, the land is quite level and receives water from French's Brook, which flows north through the lot.

The 1855 state census shows Thomas Combs and his wife, Harriet, owned a log house valued at $100. Thomas listed the cash value of the farm at $640, stock at $150, and tools and implements at $20. His 160 acres were considered unimproved because they had not been cleared of trees and rocks. The land had not been plowed or planted the previous year.[7] Thomas paid taxes of $3.54 on the property in 1855.[8]

The 1865 census states that Harriet bore ten children, but only nine children were listed throughout earlier census records: Sarah (born 1828), Rosilla (born 1830), Edward (born 1832), Alvah Coleman[9] (born 1834), Laura (born 1836), Emily (born 1840), Julia Ann[10] (born 1842), Abigail (born 1845), Harriet (born 1848).

In 1855, Thomas, Harriet, and their four daughters—Emily, age sixteen; Ann, age fifteen; Abigail, age ten; and Harriet, age seven—lived exactly where Wallace Goodspeed said Esther's family had lived. However, there is no evidence that they lived there before 1855 and they did not have a daughter named Esther.

Esther Combs would have been born in 1824 (to be fifteen in 1839). No female over the age of four is listed as offspring of Thomas Combs in the 1830 census. In 1840, Thomas Combs had two females age ten and fourteen, two males age five and nine, and two females under age four in his house. The two older girls would have been Sarah and Rosilla. It seems Thomas Combs had no daughter who was fifteen years old in 1839.

Since Thomas Combs lived in Lewis in 1840, how could Esther Combs, if she existed, have made her climb in Wilmington in 1839? One explanation is that perhaps she was visiting someone in the area. It was quite common for large families to send their children for long visits to other homes. Laura and Abigail Combs were living with another family in 1850.

The 1865 census indicated that Harriet Combs was the mother of ten children. Who was the tenth child? Could it have been a girl named Esther? In 1830, there was a five- to ten-year-old girl living with Nathan Lewis, Harriet Combs' father. Perhaps this girl was Esther.

No written evidence proves conclusively that Esther McComb or Combs existed or climbed the mountain. Writer, historian, and mountaineer Jim Goodwin cautions against drawing conclusions from the lack of written evidence: "We researchers rely too much on the written word. We must remember that few people—especially those exploring new regions—could write." Many people "probably didn't want the county office to know they were there. They were squatters. There still may be truth in the Charlie Beede story about the McCombs living on the Wilmington-Franklin Falls Road."[11]

Although written records do not tell Esther's story, they do tell Thomas Combs' story as that of an early settler trying to make a living at farming near Esther Mountain. After living near Esther Mountain for just eight years, Thomas Combs moved his family to the east side of Whiteface Mountain near Fox Farm Road.

On March 6, 1863, Thomas E. Combs sold his 160 acres on Lot #381. Russell L. French of the town of Franklin bought it for $462.50.[12] Soon Russ French would open a hotel, found a village, and blaze a trail to the top of Esther Mountain.

RUSSELL FRENCH—FIRST TRAIL BLAZER

FRENCH'S BROOK flowed down from the high slopes of Esther Mountain across the land where Thomas Comb lived for a few years and continued north past a small town known as French's, where Russell French lived his whole life.

Downstream from French's, Lincoln Brook joined French's Brook to form a large pond. The pond was known as the "pork barrel" for the large number of trout that filled it.[1] From the pond, the brooks continued into the Saranac River a few miles north of the village of McLenathan Falls (later Franklin Falls) in Franklin County.

Franklin County was formed in 1808. "It can hardly be necessary to say that this county received its name from the illustrious Franklin; and nothing was meant by attaching it to the least valuable county of this State, though the doctor, who always saw a meaning in everything, might be displeased with it should he appear here in his butt of wine,"[2] reads the *History of Clinton and Franklin County*.

In 1827, Isaac G. McLenathan and William Wells came from Jay to settle McLenathan Falls. McLenathan Falls was part of the town of Bellmont until the town of Franklin was created on May 20, 1836.

The southern part of the town of Franklin offered agricultural and industrial opportunities. Its rich soil produced plentiful crops. A magnificent forest provided sources of lumber, pulpwood, and charcoal. Along the Saranac River were excellent locations for forges, sawmills, and gristmills.

Waterfalls provided the power at McLenathan Falls. A dam, sawmill, and iron forge were the first facilities erected. An inn and store were built later. Initially, the town was not successful due to its lack of railroads and navigable waterways for exporting products. Oxen hauled lumber and iron over dirt roads to Port Kent, thirty-five miles away.

An attempt to improve transportation facilities was made in 1847. Elias Goodspeed, John Fitzgerald, and John Rogers were appointed commissioners to construct a plank road. The road was to go from McLenathan Falls to the west line of Clinton County, through the south part of Black Brook, to the Port Kent and Hopkinton Turnpike. "The road bed was leveled and heavy 3 inch planks were laid crosswise, making an excellent road for the teams and heavy hauling while it lasted. A toll gate was erected and toll collected, 25 cents—single horse, 50 cents—team, for upkeep."[3] A road sign east of Franklin Falls still designates "Plank Road."

By 1851, the McLenathan forge had changed ownership several times to finally belong to Peter Comstock, while the village had been renamed Franklin Falls. In its first appearance on a map in 1858 it was misspelled as "FANKLIN FALLS."[4]

A fire destroyed the entire village of Franklin Falls on May 29, 1852. Townspeople lost everything, barely escaping with their lives. Over fifty buildings, including the store, the school, and the hotel, burned. Unshaken, Comstock immediately began to rebuild. The sawmill was rebuilt by October and the village was quickly back in operation.

In 1852, Peter Comstock and George Tremble built a large, new hotel called The Franklin House. It was the fanciest place in the region. The famous hotel entrepreneur Paul Smith married Lydia Martin at The Franklin House in 1859.

The Franklin House stood beside the Saranac River as shown on Stoddard's map of 1883. The hotel was an immediate success, not because of the town, but because of its location. It was on the stagecoach line about halfway between Au Sable Forks and Saranac Lake.

Sportsmen, health seekers, and vacationers traditionally mounted the stage at Au Sable Forks and traveled through Black Brook, Franklin Falls, and Bloomingdale to the favored resorts of the time, Martin's at Saranac Lake and Paul Smith's at St. Regis. As the popularity of these resorts grew, The Franklin House prospered.

In 1881, Norman I. Arnold purchased The Franklin House. Norman's wife was Ann Goodspeed, daughter of Nathaniel and Polly Goodspeed, granddaughter of Elias Goodspeed, the first settler in the area. The Arnold family lived at The Franklin House in Franklin Falls for twenty years.

Three miles down the road was a settlement called French's. Luman French and Clarissa Arnold were born in Vermont in 1793 and 1795, respectively. They married and came to the region in the late 1820s. Census records show they lived in Chateaugay in 1830, Jay in 1840, and Franklin in 1850, but they probably remained on their farm on Plank Road east of McLenathan Falls, while the town and county boundary lines changed several times.

Luman and Clarissa had two sons, Samuel M., born 1833, and Russell L., born 1837. The Frenches became moderately successful farmers. By 1860, the value of their real estate was $3,000 and personal estate was $1,034. About 1863, they built and operated a sawmill on the farm.

Russ French married Anna Hewitt in 1866. They had two children, Flossie, born 1872 and Jenny, born 1874. Russ French continued to share his parents' house and to work as a farmer and lumberman. He also served as town auditor and assessor.

The Franklin House and Arnold family, about 1886. The bearded man with the white hat is Norman I. Arnold. The woman in the chair is Ann Goodspeed Arnold holding Isaac Norman Arnold.
Courtesy of Saranac Lake Free Library, Adirondack Room.

Samuel M. French and his wife, Marion S. Babbitt (1844-1914) had a daughter, Emma, born 1865, and five sons, William, born 1867, Franklin, born 1868, Frederic, born 1871, Harry, born 1872, and Henry, born 1874.

The success of The Franklin House in Franklin Falls spurred the growing French family to expand into the hotel business. They added to their house in 1872 and began taking boarders.

French's main attribute was location. The house stood where French's Brook crossed Plank Road, about three miles east of Franklin Falls. This meant it was three miles closer to Au Sable Forks than The Franklin House. After hours in a bumpy, dusty stage, travelers welcomed the first resting place.

French's was an instant success. In 1879, Stoddard wrote, "French's Hotel is the regular dining place for passengers by the stage going either way..."[5] Passengers were treated to huge plates of venison and trout and a breathtaking view of Whiteface and Esther mountains. Dinner was 75 cents; the view was free.

French's simple three-story house accommodated twenty-five guests. The stage was the center of activity; the four or six horses for the stagecoach were often switched at French's.

French's advertisement in Wallace's 1880 guidebook read:

> This House is located 3 miles east of Franklin Falls, on the Plank Road and regular Stage Route leading from Ausable Station to the Saranac and St. Regis Lakes. Dining Place for all Stages in both directions. House new and well arranged. Table furnished in first-class style.
>
> TERMS—Dinner, 75 cents; board by day, $1.50; by week, $8 to $12.
>
> ...Parties desiring a place of summer resort will find this as pleasant and healthy as any that can be found in Northern New York. Extra inducements to regular boarders, and every effort made to render their stay agreeable.[6]

As French's Hotel prospered, the settlement of French's grew. A school, store, Catholic church, and post office served the residents who included R. I. White, H. Warren, R. L. Walston, and the Frenches.[7] Because of the hotel's proximity to the mountains, the Frenches entered the booming business of guiding tourists up Whiteface and Esther mountains.

About 1859, Andrew Hickok started guiding tourists to the summit of Whiteface Mountain. According to *Forest and Crag*, Hickok's Trail was the "first definite trail" in the Adirondacks.[8] It started from his house just south of Wilmington by the fox farm. (See "A. Hecock" house near the flume on the Ausable River on French's map of 1858. Interestingly, Thomas Combs lived in a neighboring house from 1863-1867.) In *The Indian Pass*, Alfred

Street describes the trail at "the mountain's east base, where lived Hickock, who, with commendable energy, had cut a road nearly straight to the crest. In fact, it is so steep on account of its straightness, that the only wonder is he did not tumble over backward while performing his task."[9]

A party climbing the trail in August of 1859 reported:

> We soon brought up at the house of the guide, Mr. Andrew Hickock, Jr., at the foot of the mountain. The view of the stupendous height just before us was anything but encouraging in regard to the practicability of an ascent by the ladies, and those most accustomed to such undertakings shrunk back with a dread of what seemed so presumptuous an attempt as four miles of climbing up such a steep.[10]

However, they found the trail to be "excellent" and "were very happily disappointed." Upon reaching the top, Miss Hattie Wadhams became "the first lady who ever ascended White Face from the eastern side."

Around 1865, Bill Nye cut the Whiteface Brook Trail from Lake Placid. The three-and-three-fifth-mile trail reached the summit of Whiteface from the south via the slide. To get to the start of the trail, the hiker had to row six miles across Lake Placid.

A six-and-one-half-mile pony trail from Wilmington to Whiteface was built around 1870. El Hayes was in charge of this trail for Hotel Whiteface. "There were but few who rode to the summit. As we came above the timber line where the trail ran along the narrow ledges most of them lost their nerve, but the more daring rode to the summit where we staked our ponies."[11]

As described in "A Pilgrimage to John Brown's Mountain," those who attempted to climb Whiteface from the north found it was a long and hard climb through the "matted branches" and the "wreck of trees" on the north slopes.[12] This changed in 1872, when Russ and Sam French established a four-and-one-half-mile wagon trail up Whiteface Mountain from St. Armand. A two-mile foot trail continued to the summit. About a mile from the top, they built a rough camp for overnight guests.

In Wallace's guidebook, French advertised:

> "Starting point for ascent of Whiteface Mt. Carriages provided, which carry parties to within 2 miles of the summit. Total distance from hotel, 6-1/2 miles. Fare for each person, the round trip, $2. Guide for party, $3 extra, which expense can be divided among several.[13]

Whom did Russell French recommend as guide? He told Stoddard to list Wallace Goodspeed as a Whiteface Mountain guide for the Franklin Falls area. Wallace Goodspeed guided tourists up French's Trail along French's Brook and "up the natural stairway of a mountain torrent, passing secluded pools and picturesque cascades on the way."[14]

French's Trail was the easiest ascent of Whiteface. The trail appeared on Stoddard's *Map of the Adirondack Wilderness*, 1884. It also appeared on the USGS map for September 1898.

With all the trails to Whiteface, it is surprising that there is mention of only one trail to Esther Mountain in the 1800s. In *Peaks and People*, Russell Carson wrote that French cut a trail up Esther Mountain in 1866, before the Whiteface wagon trail existed. According to Jim Goodwin, "Charles Beede told Carson about a trail cut in 1866 by Russ French of French's hamlet, but gave no details as to the route. Beede climbed by this trail when he was a boy but assumed when Carson knew him that the trail had long since disappeared."[15]

French's Hotel about 1880. Note the plank road in front.
Courtesy of Adirondack Museum, Blue Mountain Lake, NY.

French's trail to the summit of Esther Mountain is not shown on any maps, probably because Whiteface quickly became a more popular destination.

Verplanck Colvin, state surveyor of the Adirondack region, apparently did not know of French's Trail or Esther Mountain. In his report of 1878, he describes an ascent from Wilmington over "the mountain next northward from Whiteface," which may be a reference to Esther.

October 11th at sunrise the party was assembled and preparations made for the ascent of Whiteface. Pack horses were procured, supplies gathered, and at noon we set out for the summit. Pushed forward with all speed, as I hoped to take advantage of the clear weather to measure and repeat to all of the new signals northward from Chazy and Cumberland Head to De Bar Mountain, and westward. We reached at dark the log camp a quarter of a mile below the summit. This was not accomplished, however, without an adventure, for in ascending the steep trail up the mountain next northward from Whiteface, one of the heavily loaded pack horses caught his foot in a root, slipped and fell headlong over a steep place, fortunately striking upon his back, which was well protected by sacks of flour and other provisions. The horse was extricated without injury, but the provisions were badly mixed. As the crest lacked a name, we now called it Pack-horse mountain.[16]

Colvin may be referring to Esther Mountain or neighboring Lookout Mountain. In 1894, Wallace recommended that on "the route passing over Pack-horse Mt." tourists should pause on the way, at "Pt. Lookout."[17] Apparently, Pack-horse Mountain became known as Lookout Mountain. Since there is no reference to Esther Mountain in Colvin's reports or notes, it is doubtful he ever climbed its summit or measured it. Likely, it was first measured to be 4,270 feet and designated "Esther Mountain" (not "Mount Esther") in 1893-94 by the United States Department of the Interior Geological Survey. Measurements from the 1978-79 USGS maps show Esther Mountain to be 4,240 feet.

Samuel French died on May 26, 1875, at age forty-one; the cause of death was listed as "Lung Feaver." His mother, Clarissa, died in 1879, at the age of eighty-four. His father, Luman, died in 1886, at the age of ninety-two. Luman, Clarissa, and Samuel are buried in the Union (Lincoln Brook) Cemetery in Franklin Falls.

Russ French continued to run French's Hotel, which continued to prosper from stagecoach travelers. As late as 1895, tourists still had to ride a stagecoach to get to the mountains. After about 1900, railroads displaced stagecoaches and the need for halfway houses like French's. In 1905, Russ French was living in the town of St. Armand, village of Forestdale. He was sixty-seven years old and working as a farmer.

French's trail up Whiteface Mountain remained in use for some time. In August 1911, Letha Mae Matteson and five others* climbed Whiteface using French's Trail.

We left Bloomingdale early in the morning, riding behind a team of bays hitched to a surrey; and drove to a farmhouse near Franklin Falls

---

* One of the others in the party was Letha's husband-to-be, Ernest R. Ryder. In 1937, he originated the name "Forty-Sixer" and became the first president of the Forty-Sixers of Troy. A new club, the Adirondack Forty-Sixers, was organized in 1948. The membership included those persons who had climbed and recorded their ascents of the forty-six mountains listed in *Peaks and People*.

S. R. Stoddard's map from 1883 accompanying his 1884 guidebook.
Three trails ascend Whiteface Mountain from: Lake Placid (3 miles),
Wilmington (6 miles), and French's (6-1/2 miles).
Courtesy Adirondack Museum, Blue Mountain Lake, NY.

at the foot of the mountain. After leaving the horses in care of the farmer, we walked along the road for about a mile to the place where the Franklin Falls trail began. One of our party had followed the trail up the mountain a few years before, so he acted as our guide. We had not traveled far when we discovered that the trail had not been kept open, and we had to climb over fallen trees and wade through brooks...[18]

In 1922, Robert Marshall wrote, "The third trail [up Whiteface] starts from French's old hotel near Franklin Falls, and follows the general course of French's Brook."[19] The 1934 Adirondack Mountain Club's *Guide to Adirondack Trails* describes the Old French Trail as a ski trail. Jim Goodwin remembers skiing it in the last week of 1931. "I had managed to drive my Model A Ford to the top of the notch on the old Wilmington-Franklin Falls road,...[then] I followed that wood road [Schwartz Trail] to the French's trail and climbed it to the top of Whiteface, descending the same way."[20]

The part of French's Trail that Jim Goodwin skied is now overgrown. It is part of the state owned McKenzie Mt. Wilderness Area. The start of French's Trail on the Wilmington-Franklin Falls Road is now privately owned and closed to the public. The Franklin House in Franklin Falls changed ownership several times. In 1892, Paul Smith bought the hotel. He closed it to the public but used it occasionally to house company employees. The house burned down in 1937.

The mills of Franklin Falls are also gone, replaced by dams built by Paul Smith's Electric Light and Power and Railroad Company. The dams flooded the "pork barrel" and several hundred acres of state land along the Saranac River, creating large reservoirs now favored by recreationists.

The village of French's is gone; the crossroads is now known as Forestdale. French's Hotel is gone; it burned down in September 1923. A surveyor's map of the property, now owned by Erika and Sal Carrara, cites the "Ruins of French's Hotel." The stone foundation and water well still lie in the woods beside the Carrara's new homestead.

All that remains to remind us of the enterprising Russell French is French's Brook. Even that has changed somewhat; it now flows under the macadam-covered Plank Road, past Forestdale, and into the Union Falls pond created by the power dam.

J. & J. ROGERS COMPANY—LANDOWNERS AND LOGGERS

AFTER OWNING IT for just eight years, Thomas Combs sold the lot at the base of Esther Mountain to Russell French. The farmer and hotelkeeper immediately sold it to the biggest landowners in the area, John and James Rogers of Au Sable Forks. The Rogers' interest was not in farming the land; they wanted the trees to make charcoal to fuel iron forges.

About 1832 Judge Halsey Rogers, his nephews James and Thomas Rogers, and John Weed arrived in Au Sable Forks. Although Halsey was a prominent judge and James and Thomas were storeowners, they were attracted to the area by the opportunities in iron. They realized that Au Sable Forks, at the forking of the Ausable River, provided a double power source for iron forges and a superb transportation facility. Wood for making charcoal and building homes could be transported from two different regions, Whiteface and Keene. Large quantities of logs could be floated down the branches of the Ausable River and plank roads could be built through areas inaccessible to the river.

Halsey bought shares in an iron business at Black Brook in the Palmer Hill area. In 1834, James, John, and Thomas bought stock in the Sable Iron Company. In 1844, Halsey Rogers adopted John Weed, who then took the name Rogers. It has been suggested that John was Halsey's illegitimate son. John Rogers married Susan B. Cowan. James Rogers married Elizabeth Hasbrouck from Hoosick Falls. They had three children: Kate (Graves), Mary (Chahoon), and Halsey, who died at age twenty. Later, James Rogers married Susan Geer and had three more children: James, Abby, and Walter. James' brother, Thomas, left the family business and Au Sable Forks.

The 1850 census showed John and James Rogers working as iron manufacturers with personal assets of $30,000 and $20,000 respectively. To expand the prospering business, they bought other iron works. In 1852, the Rogers paid $1,500 to Caleb and Emma Barton for "all of that certain piece or parcel of land and water privilege and separating machine at the Au Sable Forks...Also that other piece of land at Au Sable Forks and dwelling house."[1] In 1864, they bought Purmont iron interests at Lower Jay.

Historian Hamilton Child wrote, "This company owns about 50 coal kilns of the best construction, these being situated principally above Black Brook, many of them far up upon the slopes of the mountains that form the spurs of Whiteface and Keene Mountains. The labor of about 500 men is required to produce the coal used by this company."[2]

To fuel these operations, the Rogers began buying many acres of timberland, including lots on and around the lower slopes of Whiteface and Esther Mountains. In 1863, they bought Lots #380, #381, and #382 in St. Armand. In neighboring Wilmington they bought Lots #45 and #46 and rented Lot #47.

On March 12, 1863, Russell and Samuel French received $300 from James and John Rogers for "all the wood and timber growing, standing and lying on the south 300 acres more or less of lot number 47. . .Reserving however to the parties of the first part [the Frenches] all the pine, spruce and hemlock timber on the said 300 acres which is nine inches and over in diameter and suitable for sawing into lumber."[3] The Frenches built a mill in 1863 to saw the softwood.

The Rogers were interested in the hardwood—beech, birch, oak, and maple. They cut the hardwood, burned it, and made charcoal. Charcoal was in demand to make iron ore and to be used in forges and blacksmith shops. Making a ton of iron required at least 300 bushels of charcoal, which required about seven cords of wood.

The Rogers continued to buy forest lands. By 1871, they owned over 8,000 acres in the town of Wilmington. According to Helen Tyler's *Mountain Memories: Folk Tales of the Adirondacks*, many French Canadians, some from Montreal, came to find jobs in lumbering and charcoal. They built about thirty cabins "on the north side of the old mountain road, a little west from where the toll gate now stands." The place was called Little Montreal.[4]

The lumbermen cut up the north side of Esther Mountain with axes. Oxen and horses hauled the wood down the mountain to the charcoal kilns at West Kilns or at the base of Esther Mountain.

The upper, or west, kilns were located four miles east of Franklin Falls along Plank Road. To speed up the hauling process, a gravity railroad was built to haul the kiln wood from Little Montreal to West Kilns. The rails were hardwood two-by-fours fastened together with strips of iron and bolts. The flat-bottomed cars rolled down the hill to the kilns with a brakeman riding atop the load adjusting the pressure applied to the brakeshoes. Oxen or horses hauled the empty cars back up the hill to Little Montreal.[5]

Charcoal men mounded the wood into beehive-shaped kilns twenty to thirty feet in diameter. These first kilns were made with dirt, but later, they were built with bricks. Each kiln had a large opening at the side for inserting wood and removing charcoal. An iron door closed off the opening from drafts.

Once the brick kiln was filled with wood, it took three to five days of burning to turn the wood into charcoal. Then the charcoal was loaded onto wagons or sledges and hauled to Au Sable Forks.

Gray's 1876 map[6] shows a group of six houses along the Wilmington-Franklin Falls Road just past the present-day tollhouse; this was probably

Little Montreal. One old-timer can still point up to the site of Little Montreal in the saddle of the Stephenson Range. The gravity railroad went between the two hills, swung northward, and ended "right there by that larch tree." The end of the railroad was covered over when Plank Road was paved.[7]

The 1868 tax records for Wilmington show "Dwellings and 3 Round Kilns" with "Value: 1800" on Lot #44. The 1876 map shows these three "J. & J. Rogers Coal Kilns" at the base of Esther Mountain. Don Peterson, a local forester, located the remains of these kilns along the present Whiteface Highway. Pieces of brick and charcoal still lay beneath layers of moss and leaves.

Three more "J. & J. Rogers Coal Kilns" were located east of Morgan Pond (now Cooper Kiln Pond). These kilns probably supplied the Markham forge just south of Haselton. In 1863, James and John Rogers bought "the [Markham] forge lot being in parts of lots No. 134 + 76 Jay Tract on the Ausable in the Town of Wilmington."[8]

In Au Sable Forks, the 1876 map shows about forty-five buildings owned by "J. & J. R." It also shows their forge, store, and private residences. The *History of Clinton County, New York* describes their impressive operations:

> The J. & J. Rogers Iron Company make[s] nearly all of the charcoal used in manufacturing their iron from timber cut from their own lands, of which they own some 75,000 acres. To produce this coal it is necessary to cut the timber from 1,000 acres of land per year. This seems an immense amount of land cut over every year; but it must be remembered that timber is left to grow while the other timber is being cut, and when we remember that forty years can be allowed to grow a heavy supply of wood, it will be seen that the coal supply of this company is inexhaustible. Cutting and hauling the wood from 1,000 acres of land, burning it into coal, and hauling coal to the forges, makes a large business in itself. This company make[s] all of their own castings in their own foundry. They also run their own grist-mill, lath-mill, and shingle-mill. They burn lime, make brick, build and own nearly all of the houses in which their workmen live; they make their own wagons and all their own machinery, including lathes for their machine-shop; build steam-engines; they have three stores in which they retail $350,000 worth of goods per year; do nearly all their own teaming; own and keep thirty odd miles of plank-road in repair, and still have energy enough left to occasionally experiment with a horse-nail machine or a deoxidizing furnace.[9]

James and John Rogers ran the business under their own names until December 29, 1870, when they incorporated as J. & J. Rogers Iron Company, with James as president and John as vice-president. In 1877, James "Dandy Jim" Rogers became ill and retired as president of the company. He died

January 9, 1880. He was remembered as a thorough, cautious, and far-seeing business man whose company was at the cutting edge of technology and produced the finest cast steel and iron in the world. He was remembered for his "cheerful and sunny face, his genial manners, his uniform politeness, his kindly sympathy."[10]

By 1886, most of the Rogers' land was classified as "denuded" or "waste." The four major lumbering areas were along BonnieView Avenue in Wilmington, on the north slopes of Esther Mountain, along the western part of the Stephenson Range, and in the White Brook and Marble Mountain area. On the western side of Esther Mountain, the Esther Brook area was only "denuded in part."[11]

In the late 1880s, the Rogers Company iron operation was hurting because of increased price competition and technological advancements. By 1889, the entire operation was shut down and many out-of-work laborers left town. In *An Industrial History of Au Sable Forks New York*, Elsa C. Voelcker, granddaughter of Henry Geer Rogers, describes how other families survived by picking blueberries from the recently logged areas. Two of the Rogers boys started a berry business. They shipped the berries to Albany, enabling the townspeople to make enough money to get through the winter.[12]

In 1893, the Rogers brothers redirected their resources to the paper industry. A method had been devised a few years earlier for manufacturing paper from wood pulp instead of cloth rags. They built a new sawmill and pulp mill in Au Sable Forks and a large paper mill on the Ausable River in Jay. The J. & J. Rogers Iron Company became the J. & J. Rogers Company and remained one of the largest and most prosperous companies in the state at that time.

The new mill produced its first pulp on June 10, 1894. By August, it was making and selling twenty tons of pulp each day. Lumbering activities expanded greatly since logs of any softwood, of any size, could be used in these new pulpwood operations. Over the next twenty years, the company acquired and harvested large tracts of land consuming an estimated 50,000 cords of wood per year.

As they exhausted the more accessible resources, the Rogers Company began to log virgin forests on the higher mountain slopes. They started to cut trees on the upper slopes of Whiteface and Esther mountains about 1918.

The trees were cut into four-foot lengths of pulp. A road (now Schwartz Trail) was used to haul the wood from the slopes of the mountain to the banks of a small pond just below the present-day tollhouse. Most of the hauling was done in the winter by horses pulling sleds holding eight cords of wood.

One problem remained: how to get the logs the three miles from the holding pond down to the Ausable River. Hauling the wood *down* the steep

Log flume emptying into the Ausable River near Wilmington (from *History of the Lumber Industry in the State of New York* by William F. Fox, 1901).

hill would have been too dangerous, so they built a flume and slid the logs down the mountain.

The Rogers Company built a water trough about three miles long on the eastern side of Esther. A dam, built from stone undoubtedly from the quarry across the road, held back the water. When the water was released, it filled the trough with a shallow stream. The four-foot pulp logs were pushed one-by-one into the water slide. The trough carried the pulp stock down the mountain, across Red Brook, under the road, and into the West Branch of the Ausable River at Wilmington (near the present-day Sportsman's Inn). Lumbermen drove the logs ten miles down the river to the pulp mills in Au Sable Forks.

This was not the first water trough in the Esther Mountain area. Pictures from about 1900 show three or four different troughs. One photograph shows logs dropping from the end of the water slide into the Ausable River. It is believed this slide was later used as the terminus of the Red Brook slide. Doug Wolfe of Wilmington recalls, "My mother used to live next to it in 1921. Some kids slid in the trough but she was not allowed near it. It usually had residual water in it. . .and lots of splinters."

Elsa Voelcker states that the Rogers Company had three slips on Whiteface and two slips in the Keene area. Photograph 6 in the "Making Pulp" section of Voelcker's book appears to be of the Red Brook trough described previously.[13] Recently, Don Peterson, located the trough path, two sideboards, and two support posts along Red Brook. A second trough path, discovered by the author, heads upslope from Red Brook.

The cutting of pulp wood drastically scarred the area. Old and young trees were cut. Poplar and spruce were cut. Then hemlock, pine, and balsam were cut. "This close cutting of the spruce and other kinds left no provision for future growth, and thinned the forest so severely in places that further damage was inflicted by winds and ice storms," remarked William Fox in *History of the Lumber Industry*.[14]

These clear-cutting practices completely denuded the White Brook valley between Esther and Marble Mountains. Tremendous amounts of peeled bark and slash accumulated in the woods, creating an ugly sight and a fire hazard.

Eventually, J. & J. Rogers Co. began buying pulpwood from Canada and selling most of its land around Esther Mountain, Whiteface Mountain, and High Falls Gorge to the State of New York. Most of the land had been clear-cut, but some had not.

In January 1921, the state paid $393,040 for the north half of Whiteface Mountain, which included over 2,200 acres. This conveyance was "subject to a right of way across said lot for a wagon road and a railroad to the top of Whiteface Mountain."[15] In June 1921, the state bought the peaks of Esther and Lookout Mountains, which included over 1,900 acres. Most importantly, this purchase included the Esther Brook basin, covered with old growth spruce and fir.

In 1928, the state paid $70,307 for over 5,000 acres around Esther Mountain and the Stephenson Range. In another transaction on March 22, 1930, J. & J. Rogers Company sold 2,560 acres to the State of New York for $19,260. This parcel of land included the lower northwest slopes of Esther Mountain and Lot #381, previously owned by Thomas Combs and Russell French.

In 1955, the J. & J. Rogers Company was sold to a large corporation. Over the succeeding years, the pulp mill closed, the union went on a long strike, and the government imposed numerous water pollution controls. Diminishing profits and the impending expense of upgrading the facility forced the paper mill to close in February of 1971. The 140-year-old business was gone and so were the jobs of most people in Au Sable Forks.

Just as millions of years ago Esther Mountain recovered from glacial scraping and scouring, it would now regenerate its forests and wildlife. Old spruce and fir trees and young birch and balsam trees would be left "forever wild," protected by Article VII, Section 7 of the New York State Constitution. Esther Mountain would be preserved as part of the largest forest reservation in the nation.

The "holding pond."
Photo by the author.

RUSSELL CARSON—FIRST HISTORIAN

EXCEPT FOR Esther Combs, Russ French, and the Rogers Company's lumbermen, people largely ignored Esther Mountain through the nineteenth century. In the early twentieth century, it became state land and hikers discovered Esther Mountain as a high peak.

In 1922, the newly formed Adirondack Mountain Club issued its first publication, a pamphlet by Robert Marshall titled *The High Peaks of the Adirondacks*. It contained "a brief account of the climbing of the forty-two Adirondack mountains over 4,000 feet in height by an amateur mountain climber for fellow amateurs."[1]

Marshall's pamphlet listed Esther at 4,270 feet high and ranked its view very poorly, thirty-eight out of forty-two. It contained the first published account of a climb up Esther Mountain:

> We cut up this mountain through some very bad slash from the Wilmington Trail up Whiteface. The view in no way compensated us for the trouble. We could see slash toward Bloomingdale, slash toward the Wilmington Range, slash toward the open fields along the Ausable. We could see some of the high mountains in the distance to the south. The best part of the view was Whiteface, towering up directly to the southwest.[2]

The "we" refers to Robert Marshall, his brother, George Marshall, and their guide, Herb Clark. The "slash" refers to the small branches and treetops littering the land, likely a result of the lumbering done by J. & J. Rogers Company from 1918 to 1921.

After reading Marshall's pamphlet, Russell Mack Little Carson began researching the "how, when, and why" of the names of the Adirondack high peaks. He wrote about forty-six peaks, Marshall's forty-two plus four others over 4,000 feet that Marshall had not yet climbed. Carson's research was published in 1927 as *Peaks and People*.

Russ Carson's intensive research uncovered many unknown and previously undocumented details about first ascents and mountain namesakes. However, Carson found Esther's origin "the most obscure of any of the forty-two listed by Robert Marshall."[3] When Carson wrote to local guides and historians asking about Esther Mountain, he received replies such as, "Mt. Esther. I do not know this mt. or its location. Know nothing about it, in fact, and doubt if any person in this section does,"[4] and "Esther is a new one on me. The first mountain north of Whiteface was called Stores."[5]

Russell Carson.
Courtesy of Shirley Kendall.

Even with the aid of Robert and George Marshall, Scott Brown, T. Morris Longstreth, and others, the origin of Mt. Esther's name was perplexing. The first guess was that Russ French, the first person to cut a trail to Mt. Esther, had named it.

In a letter dated April 4, 1923, Scott Brown told Carson about discovering the 1858 map of Essex County showing Mount Esther. "This map shows Mt. Esther as plain as can be. . . .I conclude the Mt. first took [the] name, Esther, back as early as Marcy, etc., did,"[6] since other mountains named on the 1858 map (Whiteface, Dix, Giant of the Valley, Wallface, etc.) had been given names in early times. Brown suggested that French simply *renamed* the mountain Esther when he cut a trail in 1866.

Why would French have named it Esther? There appears to be no one named Esther in the French family. Neither the census records nor the local cemeteries list an Esther French.

Robert Marshall wrote that he thought he heard somewhere that Esther was named after the wife of one of the Rogers of the J. & J. Rogers Company.[7] When questioned, none of the Rogers knew anything about this. Much current literature has been written about the Rogers family and their company. There is no mention of an Esther.

In a letter dated May 26, 1923, Carson notes, "French's *Gazetteer*, 1860, mentions that Esther Kellogg was the first school teacher in Wilmington and we are wondering if perhaps the mountain might have been named for her. It is only a wild guess however."[8] Carson found no more information about her.

Several history books mention Esther Kellogg as the first teacher in Wilmington and assume she was teaching around 1815. No additional details about her have been found.

Carson's leads were incredibly disappointing. Scott Brown reported that he had written over twenty-five letters and talked to many people about Esther and he had no more leads; it seemed hopeless. Then, on November 11, 1923, Carson wrote back to Brown, "We thought we were skunked on this name but here it is:"[9]

> The story Charlie Beede told me about Esther is as follows. About 1849 a family named Macomb lived at the foot of the mountain on the road from Wilmington to St. Armand. They had a daughter Esther who was anxious to climb the mountain and one day attempted it alone. She became lost and searching parties were on the mountain all night searching for her. She was found in the morning none the worse for her experience. The mountain began to be called Esther from that event. This version was told to Beede by Wallace Goodspeed, 88 years old, who was born and brought up at St. Armand, and now lives near Potsdam. Isn't that great.[10]

Walter P., Ed Phelps, Alan Beede, Julia Beede, Charlie Beede, Russ Beede
at the Beede sugar camp, about 1900.
Courtesy of Keene Valley Library.

This letter is almost word for word what was printed in *Peaks and People* (see Esther Combs chapter). The two differences are the date, which reads 1849 in the letter and 1839 in the book, and the spelling of the name, which reads Macomb in the letter and McComb in the book. Carson later refers to "Esther Combs" and Beede writes the name as "Esther Coombs." In other notes and letters, the name Macomb is crossed out and changed to Combs. For some reason, McComb was printed in the book.

Certainly the story that Charlie Beede obtained from Wallace Goodspeed was the most plausible and authentic. Both men were revered as great Adirondack guides. Wallace Goodspeed was a descendent of the first settlers at the base of Esther Mountain. He was born there in 1839, raised his family there, and guided tourists up Whiteface Mountain in the 1880s. Undoubtedly, Wallace Goodspeed knew the history and folklore of the area.

Charlie Beede was born in 1855 in Essex County. His father, Orren Beede, died in 1864 in the Civil War. His mother, Lydia E. Lincoln, became known as the Second Widow Beede. The First Widow Beede was Charlie's grandmother Diadamia, wife of Phineas Beede.

Charlie Beede married Luna Corintha Phelps, daughter of Orson "Old Mountain" Phelps and Lorinda Lamb. Charlie and Luna had four children: Edna, Russ, Alan "Baddy," and Julia. As the son-in-law and neighbor of the notorious guide Old Mountain Phelps and the brother-in-law, business partner, and friend of Ed Phelps, Beede undoubtedly knew all of the local tales and legends.

Carson was satisfied with the story Beede had relayed from Wallace Goodspeed about the name origin. However, had Esther actually reached the summit? It seems unlikely that a lost girl would push her way through the thick, scratchy balsam to get to the summit. Should Esther Combs be credited with the first ascent of the mountain? Beede answered, "I do not know whether Esther Coombs reached the summit of Mount Esther or not."[11]

Since Carson had no better alternative, he reasoned, "Perhaps that may come to the attention of somebody who can go back further and it may draw out some information that can be used in a revision if the book ever gets to that point."[12]

Today, mountaineers familiar with Esther Mountain insist that there is no way to climb through the thick brush on the north face of Esther. They claim that it is simply impassable. However, is anything impassable to a determined fifteen-year-old?

Another possible name source was presented to Carson on December 6, 1924. Bob Marshall wrote Carson to relay a story he had heard from his roommate at Harvard Forest College, who had heard it from a man in the Bloomingdale region. "This man claimed that he had been to Albany three times to get the name of Esther changed to Estes, after an old settler who had lived on the side of the mountain years before, and after whom he claimed the mountain had really been named."[13]

Marshall's roommate "was not very much impressed," and dismissed the story as a tall tale told to impress a visitor. Carson, too, discounted the story.

To think that the only mountain believed to be named for a woman may, in fact, be named for a man is most disturbing. At first, it seems unlikely that Estes could be confused with Esther. However, when New Englanders spoke they often added an "er" to names. Estes might have been pronounced "Ester" and this would explain the confusion.

The best known Estes in the region was Otis Estes of Keene Valley. He supposedly named Big Slide Mountain. Otis Estes came from Vermont about 1800 and was one of the earliest settlers of Keene Valley.

Otis's son, Otis Estes, Jr., was born in the town of Keene on June 3, 1814. He married Rhoda Ann (Lamb) Merrill on September 19, 1839. They also resided on the Estes farm. In a corner of the farm property, now owned by descendants of Reverend Livingston Ludlow Taylor, is the Estes family cemetery. It holds the graves of Otis Estes, Jr., Rhoda Ann Estes, and Orson "Old Mountain" Phelps.

Old Mountain Phelps and Beede were close neighbors of the Esteses. Surely, Beede would have known if Esther Mountain was named for Otis Estes or Otis Estes Jr.

Esther Combs (or McComb) remained the most plausible name origin for the mountain. As Carson suggested, perhaps somebody could go back and uncover more information about the name origin. Finding written evidence is difficult, however, because Esther was female, and prior to 1850, federal censuses listed only heads of household—usually males. Esther was probably married before 1850, so her maiden name would not appear in a census listing. Birth, marriage, and death records are sketchy or non-existent. Cemetery stones are missing, unreadable, or non-existent for common folk. Few women are mentioned in history books.

After extensive searching, written evidence revealed four other possiblities: Esther Phelps, Esther Lathrop, Esther Weston, or Esther (Preston) Hayes.

In 1830, Orin Phelps and Ruth Schofield Phelps moved from Vermont to Schroon. From there they moved to Horicon in Warren County. Their twelve children included Esther M. and Orson "Old Mountain" Phelps. Esther was born in Vermont on November 12, 1814. She married William Foster and had three daughters, including Esther Elvira, born April 20, 1834. Esther Phelps died February 19, 1838, and was buried in South Schroon, one year before the Esther Mountain climb.

In 1839, Esther Elvira Foster would have been five years old. Thus it seems implausible that either Esther Phelps or Esther Foster is the namesake of the mountain.

Esther and William Lathrop lived in St. Armand, near Bloomingdale, in 1850. The census records show: William Lathrop, age 32, farmer; Esther, age 23, born in New York; Harriet, age 5; Andrew, age 2; and Clarissa, age 10 months.

The same family is listed in the 1850 census in the town of Franklin, county of Franklin. In that listing, the 23 year-old-female is named Jane E.; Esther must have been her middle name.

Donaldson's *History of the Adirondacks* says that Azel Lathrop, William's father, came from Vermont and arrived in St. Armand in 1850. Azel, his wife, and their ten children lived on 160 acres, which later became the site of Trudeau's Sanatorium. By the mid-1860s, the family left and moved out West. A town called Lathrop sprang up outside Escanaba, Michigan.[14]

Jane Esther Lathrop's maiden name could have been Combs or McComb, but, she would have been only twelve in 1839. She could have grown up near French's Brook, but in 1850 she was living on the other side of the mountain.

The other two Esthers lived near Wilmington. This makes it plausible for them to have reached the summit of the mountain via a route from the east near the current-day trail. Most old-timers assume Esther climbed from near the present-day Santa's Workshop along the ridge above Marble Mountain.

In 1845, Essex County recorded a deed to Harry Weston of Wilmington of Lot #15 of Jay Tract (behind Hayes Cemetery). Birth records for 1849 show the birth of a daughter, Ann Augusta, to Harry and Esther Weston of Wilmington. Harry (age 36) and Esther (age 29) appear in the 1850 census for Wilmington. By 1855, Esther was widowed with four children. Esther Weston would have been eighteen in 1839, a bit older than the girl in the story.

The other possibility is Esther (Preston) Hayes, born August 29, 1827. In 1845 she married David B. Hayes. In *The History of Essex County*, David B. Hayes is listed as a prominent citizen. He was born in 1822 in Jay and was a hammersman at the forge. Birth records show a son Ellsworth was born to Esther and David Hayes in 1848 in Wilmington. Esther died in 1868, leaving three children.

Esther is buried next to Hiram Preston in the Hayes Cemetery. In 1830, the Prestons lived along the Bonnie View Road behind the present-day Santa's Workshop. This makes it plausible for Esther to have reached the mountain, although she was only twelve years old in 1839.

For whom was Esther Mountain named? Who made the first climb? Was it a young girl named Esther McComb, or Esther Combs, or Esther Preston? Was it a schoolteacher? A man named Estes? Russell Carson posed those questions when he started to research Esther Mountain. He followed many trails to many fascinating destinations, but none led to Esther.

Russell Carson gave Esther Mountain a marvelous legend and an intriguing mystery. And he gave the Adirondacks much more. Carson served the Adirondack Mountain Club as president in 1930-31. He also served as chairman of his chapter and as a member of the club's board of governors, and helped to establish the club's first magazine, *High Spots*. He was a trustee of the Association for the Protection of the Adirondacks for more than twenty years. In 1935 he served on the executive committee of the New York State Commission on Fifty Years of Conservation.

Carson was a life-long collector of Adirondackana. Before he died on January 7, 1961, at the age of seventy-six, he donated his collection of some 600 books and pamphlets to the Adirondack Historical Association. This became the start of the Adirondack Museum Library at Blue Mountain Lake.

Perhaps somewhere among his books are unturned pages with trails leading to Esther.

GRACE HUDOWALSKI—FIRST STEWARD

"She pushed on through brush and tall trees, scaled bump after bump and pulled herself over ledges until she finally stood atop her mountain...she had climbed a mountain—for pleasure. Unheard of! For adventure. Incredible!"[1] Those are the words Grace Hudowalski used to describe her vision of Esther McComb's climb.

Like Esther, Grace Hudowalski climbed her first peak at age fifteen. That climb up Marcy in 1921 hooked Grace on the mountains. On August 28, 1937, Grace became the ninth member, and first woman member, of the Forty-Sixers of Troy by climbing Esther Mountain. She had specifically saved Esther for last!

Climbers in the 1920s and 1930s considered Esther Mountain a difficult trailless peak. With C. Howard Nash, Grace wrote: "Her slash-covered sides, dead down timber and very thick balsam present numerous pitfalls to the hiker who seeks her summit...Finally the hiker pushes through thick slash and up dwarf balsam to a small bare rock top encircled by more balsam, Esther's summit. It is perhaps one of the roughest climbs in the mountains, certainly not at all ladylike."[2]

In 1922, Robert Marshall, George Marshall, and Herb Clark (the first Forty-Sixers) ranked the view from Esther's summit as thirty-eight out of forty-two because of the surrounding slash. In 1939, Robert Marshall, then renowned as a conservationist and founder of The Wilderness Society, wrote to Grace:

> I should think that since this is still a trailless peak it might be fun to get up a group climb of this peak sometime during the summer to commemorate Esther McComb and her remarkable initiative which resulted in the only first ascent of a high Adirondack peak by a woman and the first mountain to be climbed for the reason which instigates practically all Adirondack mountain climbing nowadays.[3]

Grace and Ed "Hudo" Hudowalski and the Forty-Sixers of Troy organized a centennial climb of Esther Mountain. They brought with them a bronze plaque made by Margery Nash Ludlow of Troy to be placed on Esther's summit. Grace chose the memorable words:

```
     1839   MT. ESTHER   1939
              4270 FEET
           TO COMMEMORATE
      THE INDOMITABLE SPIRIT OF
            ESTHER MCCOMB
                AGE 15
     WHO MADE THE FIRST RECORDED
         ASCENT OF THIS PEAK
               FOR THE
       "SHEER JOY OF CLIMBING"
         TROY      46R      N.Y.
```

On Saturday morning, July 29, 1939, one group of hikers climbed north to Whiteface Mountain from Whiteface Landing at the end of Lake Placid. Other hikers met them at the top and spent the night at the Wilmington leanto just below the summit of Whiteface. (Unfortunately, Robert Marshall was in Alaska so he could not attend. He died later that year.)

On Sunday morning, Clarence Craver led a sunrise service in the mist. The service included a scripture reading from Psalm 121, prayers, and two songs, "This Is My Fathers World" and "My Country, 'Tis Of Thee."

Following the service, the group ate breakfast at the Whiteface Castle. About noon, the party of twenty or so hikers began their pilgrimage by descending the Wilmington trail to the east. After a short distance, they went off in a northeasterly direction, bushwacking to Esther's summit.

Grace led the ceremony at the peak of Esther Mountain. She began by recounting her interest in Esther:

> At one time Esther meant absolutely nothing to me. Had you said her name I would have thought of a beautiful Jewish maiden wed to a Persian King back in the B.C. days. The maiden stands for much bravery and courage. She was the go-get-what-you-want type of girl and she did get what she went for. (Not unlike the little miss for whom this peak is named!)
>
> Then, in the June 1936 issue of "Epworth Embers,"[4] a publication with which our 46-ers are familiar, there appeared an article stating that on a certain Sunday in that year, five young men had climbed Esther. The article was lengthy and it very graphically depicted the plodding and pushing, the underbrush, windfalls and dense growth of pine; a bump that wasn't the top at all. The account ended with these words, "With almost final breath we got to the summit, flopped our weary bones on the softest looking rock, expended what feeble strength remained in a fruitless attempt to keep off flies and punkies, weakly but unitedly shouted, 'Hurrah, we've made Esther!' "
>
> Three of the five on that party are here today. From the tales those fellows told about "making Esther" three years ago I gathered she was

some gal! In fact then and there I decided that if it should be my lot to climb all the 46 major peaks I would finish on Esther.

And such was my lot! Esther may be tough and full of downfalls to the hiker who seeks to ascend her, but she is a special favorite of mine.

It was late afternoon of a late August day two years ago that I came through the trees and pulled myself rather exultantly to this spot. It had tried to rain all the way over, but by the time I reached the top the sun had broken through the clouds and the most radiant, colorful rainbow curled itself around Esther's head, truly making her a pot of gold for me. She was my 46th peak! It was Holy Ground here!

Perhaps you can realize with what joy it is that I stand here today, and doubly happy I am to see that there are those who are not afraid to PUSH their way to the mountain tops.[5]

A few short speeches followed and then Miss Eleanor M. Plum, chairman of the Albany Chapter of the Adirondack Mountain Club, unveiled the plaque that Ed Hudowalski, president of the Forty-Sixers, had cemented to the summit. A. S. Hopkins, Assistant Director of Lands and Forests in the New York State Conservation Department, spoke informally at the ceremony, covered with scratches and torn trousers. Evidently, the cripple brush had done its job!

The program closed with the singing of a tribute to the little girl named Esther. The song was composed for the centennial by Grace and Clarence.

To Esther McComb

O, Esther! Spirit-brave!
O, Maid! Undaunted, true!
We pay our homage and respect
Upon this mount to you!

Not for renown or fame
You climbed this rugged peak;
But for the joy of drinking in
The virgin beauty deep.

Long may thy spirit flame
In hearts of everyone!
Long may thy deed inspire, O Maid,
Who climbed here just for fun!*

---

* Grace L. Hudowalski and Clarence R. Craver (sung at Esther Centennial 1939 to the tune of "St. Thomas").

After the singing, "Goodbyes were said and the party broke up for the homeward scoot," according to *The August Reporter*, published by the Albany Chapter of the Adirondack Mountain Club.[6]

The centennial plaque still marks the summit of Esther Mountain. When it became loose recently, Ed Ketchledge reset it.

Grace Hudowalski is a champion and matron of the Adirondack Mountains. She served as the first president of the Adirondack Forty-Sixers and has been the first and only historian of the club. She corresponds with every aspiring and accomplished Forty-Sixer, writing over 1,600 letters annually.

Grace can no longer climb Esther Mountain and sign in at the summit canister, so the summit canister came to her. One of Grace's prized possessions is the original Esther Mountain summit canister which she uses to hold her Forty-Sixer guest book at Boulders, her summer camp in the Adirondacks.

Esther Mountain Centennial Celebration in 1939. The bandana-covered plaque is about to be revealed. Grace Hudowalski is in the middle wearing a plaid shirt. She wrote to the author: "I still have it, worn and motheaten." Arthur Hopkins is in the ripped, white pants. Courtesy of Grace Hudowalski.

NEW DEVELOPMENTS

AS ESTHER MOUNTAIN was gaining the attention of hikers, Whiteface Mountain was drawing the attention of developers: road erectors, ski center builders, and theme park planners. The faces of Whiteface and Esther Mountains started changing in 1927 when New Yorkers approved an amendment to Article VII, Section 7, of the New York State Constitution. The amendment granted the building of a highway on "forever wild" lands. The road would cut across the side of Esther Mountain, within a half mile of its wilderness summit, and continue to the top of Whiteface Mountain.

The road's purpose was to provide access to the summit view on Whiteface. Not only climbers and hikers, but thousands of motorists could enjoy the beautiful view from the fifth highest peak in the state.

"But this ambition requires a closer analysis than it has yet received," argued George Horace Lorimer, editor of *The Saturday Evening Post*. He continued:

> The assumption that views from mountain peaks are necessarily more rewarding than from other points is not borne out by the facts...Who really dares say that the view from a mountain peak is finer than the view of the mountain itself?...Yet the voters of a great state actually amend their basic law, the very constitution itself, to permit the building of a road...for a purpose which is both unnecessary and in line with the gradual whittling away of one of the State's supreme heritages.[1]

The American Legion campaigned for the highway, which was to be dedicated as a memorial to the New York war veterans. "That is, however, a mere pretext, and in reality an insult to those who fought in the war," wrote Louis Marshall in a letter to the editor of *The New York Times*. "Today White Face without a road constitutes a finer tribute than any number of artificial monuments which tend to destroy the harmony of nature...Let us preserve some of the simple things. Let us know that there is somewhere in our State a region which is not commercialized and citified..."[2]

Russell Carson asked, "...is it [Whiteface Road] worthwhile at the expense of tinkering with a law that was won only after such a hard and long fight?"[3] The voters of the State of New York replied *YES* and the highway was built.

On September 11, 1929, Governor Franklin D. Roosevelt dug the first shovel of dirt to symbolize the beginning of construction of Whiteface Mountain Veterans Memorial Highway. Actual road construction began on Christmas Day 1931, but winter weather immediately slowed work. Severe weather forced a shutdown from December 1932 to May 1933 and again from November 1933 to May 1934. "A suggestion of the weather conditions that faced the contractors is given by the statement that snow falls on Whiteface summit practically every month in the year, that ice has been encountered in rock cuts as late as July, and that once, in the winter of 1932-33, drilling and blasting operations were carried on in 40-below zero temperatures."[4]

Hagedorn Contracting Company, Inc. was the construction contractor for the project. The road was to be 32 feet wide (ditch-to-ditch) and have an average grade of 8-1/2 percent. The alignment called for two hairpin turns near the top of the mountain. Also, a toll gate was to be constructed three miles from Wilmington.[5]

It took four years and $1,250,000 to build the road and associated structures. The highway opened on July 20, 1935, and over 17,000 people traveled to the summit in the first month. On September 14, President Roosevelt returned to the site to dedicate the highway as a memorial to those of New York State killed in the World War. The toll for use of the highway was one dollar per passenger. From the top, you could see all the peaks and rivers and lakes and clouds. This view inspired President Roosevelt's famous slogan, "See the Adirondacks for a Dollar!"

The two-lane highway, known as State Highway 431, is eight miles long and climbs 3,400 feet. The tolled portion of the road starts at the chalet-style gate house overlooking Lake Stevens.* The road climbs gently as it cuts across the lower slopes of Esther Mountain. It crosses Esther Brook within one-half mile of Esther Mountain's summit and then crosses branches of French's Brook as it winds around the west face of Esther Mountain and continues south onto Whiteface Mountain. The road ends at the Whiteface Castle, just 276 feet from the summit. The castle, constructed of the mountain's granite, houses a snack bar and gift shop.

Visitors can reach the summit by climbing a stone stairway or by riding an elevator. The twenty-seven-story elevator is reached by walking through a 424-foot-long tunnel carved out of the granite. Inside the rock tunnel, the temperature remains between 39 and 43 degrees every day of the year.[6]

A 360-degree panorama can be enjoyed at the mountain top. There are views of Lake Champlain and Vermont's Green Mountains to the east, the St. Lawrence Valley and Canada to the north, Lake Placid and the High Peaks to the south, and the Saranac Lake valley to the west. There is a fabulous view of Esther Mountain to the northeast.

---

*Although Lake Stevens is man-made, it is a living museum of high-elevation lake vegetation.

Parts of the summit buildings were used for the Whiteface Mountain Meteorological Observatory. The College of Engineering of New York University in New York City and Rensselaer Polytechnic Institute in Troy, New York, shared equally in the observatory's expenses and maintenance. S. M. Serebreny, Director of the Observatory in 1938, wrote, "Essentially ours is a meteorological observatory for the express purpose of collecting and disseminating the observational data, co-operating with other like stations in furthering various studies possible in mountain meteorology; hopeful of evolving new techniques..."[7] The observatory participated in various ozone and radio wave studies until it closed in 1946.

Interest in Whiteface Mountain as a ski area was aroused even before Whiteface Highway was completed. One of the cross-country ski trails for the 1932 Winter Olympics circled Whiteface and Esther Mountains. Narrow trails were considered legal on state-owned Forest Preserve land at that time.

The 29.5-mile ski loop started from the west shore of Lake Placid, headed north, and crossed the old Lincoln Pond trail that led to Franklin Falls via the Goodspeed homestead. Then it headed southeast toward Whiteface. After a short climb, it turned north, crossed French's Trail, and traveled along the Schwartz trail, created for J. & J. Rogers Company lumbering operations. Jim Goodwin recalls skiing this part of the trail in 1931: "Reaching the spot where the toll house now exists, we were given a choice of climbing what had been a lumber road some 3 or 4 hundred feet up on Esther from which a hairy descent brought us back to the more conservative skiers, waiting at the toll site. Then we all skied down the primitive—of course unplowed—road down to Wilmington..."[8]

The Olympic ski trail wound around Marble Mountain, down toward the Ausable River, past Sunrise Notch and Connery Pond, and into Lake Placid stadium. It was never used in Olympic competition due to warm temperatures on race day.

In 1938, a ski racing trail was built on Little Whiteface Mountain on land owned by J. & J. Rogers Company. Skiers raced two miles down through the woods and then walked back up the mountain. Many New York skiers grew tired of walking up hills or traveling to other states and wanted a large-scale ski center in the Adirondacks.

On November 4, 1941, New Yorkers voted on an amendment to allow construction of ski trails on Forest Preserve land on Whiteface Mountain. The amendment to Article XIV, Section 1 (previously Article VII, Section 7) of the State Constitution was as follows:

> The lands of the State, now owned or hereafter acquired, constituting the Forest Preserve as now fixed by law, shall be forever kept as wild forest lands. They shall not be leased, sold, or exchanged, or be taken by any corporation, public or private, nor shall timber thereon be sold,

removed or destroyed. Nothing herein contained shall prevent the State from constructing, completing and maintaining any highway heretofore specifically authorized by constitutional amendment, nor from constructing and maintaining not more than twenty miles of ski trails thirty to eighty feet wide on the north, east and northwest slopes of Whiteface Mountain in Essex County.

The south slopes, facing Lake Placid, were explicitly excluded from the amendment. All trails were to be located on the slopes near the highway and constructed such that they would be practically invisible during spring, summer, and fall.

Why Whiteface? Advocates of a YES vote pointed out that Whiteface Mountain was no longer wild; a highway had been blasted through the mountain and already scarred the view from the north. Whiteface offered accessibility by a third of the nation's population, highway transportation to the top, a long skiing season due to its reliable snow cover, and a range in slopes from gentle to steep.

Those opposing the amendment believed a ski center would result in encroachments in other parts of the Forest Preserve, the further destruction of the remaining wilderness values of Whiteface Mountain, and soil erosion. They also believed the planned ski center would not serve the *average* skier, and was a direct attack on New York State Constitution.

The amendment was approved 740,506 to 730,562. "It just scraped through," said Hal Burton. "The city vote did the trick. The farmers were against it."[9]

With the outbreak of World War II, construction of the ski center was put on hold. In 1944, plans for the ski center were revised to develop the Marble Mountain area instead of the area on the east slopes of Whiteface.

In the winter of 1948-49, the Whiteface Mountain Ski Center opened with a T-bar lift on Marble Mountain and a lodge at the base between Esther and Marble mountains. A chairlift up Esther was proposed but never built. Instead, trucks and Sno-Cats took skiers to trails off the Whiteface highway at the 4,000-foot level. The trails led down the northeast side of Whiteface toward Esther. The area between Whiteface, Esther, and Lookout was full of cross-country and alpine ski trails and snowmobile roads.

A ski lodge stood at the top of Lookout Mountain; its charred remains and cement foundation still lay along the trail. From the Lookout ski lodge, one trail spur led north to Esther's summit. Jim Goodwin recalls starting at the other trailhead, "from which, with good snow conditions, an 'Inferno Race' was run from there to the bottom of Marble Mountain."[10]

The main lodge at the bottom of the mountain was built of cypress with a knotty pine interior. It burned on May 6, 1951. Reconstruction began on August 1, using logs salvaged from the blowdown of November 25, 1950. A special variance was granted to allow the blowdown debris on Forest

Preserve land to be sold and removed. The Conservation Department reasoned that the removal of the downed trees would prevent serious fires.

Spruce logs, up to eighteen inches in diameter, were hauled from Pigeon Roost near the Goodspeed's homestead. That area had been hit by hurricane winds exceeding 100 miles per hour. Despite poor roads and heavy snows, the salvage operation removed large quantities of timber. The lodge was ready for use by December 15 of the same year.

Unfortunately, the ski area was plagued by perpetual winds, icy slopes, and minimal snow cover. Skiers were unhappy and the facility was losing money.

In 1957, the state legislature approved the allocation of $2.5 million to complete development of a ski center on the east face of Whiteface and Little Whiteface. On January 25, 1958, Governor W. Averill Harriman dedicated the new Whiteface Mountain Ski Center. The old Marble Mountain Ski Center fell out of use; it did not even open the winter of 1959-60.

Whiteface Mountain Ski Center prospered. In 1966, after a major expansion, Whiteface could claim the highest vertical drop in the East—3,216 feet. Additional improvements were made for the 1980 Winter Olympic Games. In 1994, Whiteface was ranked the top ski resort in the Northeast by readers of the magazine *Snow Country*. The article concluded: "Whiteface Mountain stands head and shoulders above all other ski areas."[11]

Each winter, thousands of skiers race down Whiteface Mountain. After the snow has melted, people still flock to the area—not to go skiing, but to visit Santa Claus. From May to December Santa lives at North Pole, New York, on the east side of Esther Mountain.

Santa's Workshop was the first roadside attraction along Whiteface Highway. It opened in the summer of 1949. Julian Reiss and Harold Fortune of Lake Placid and Arto Monaco of Upper Jay started the park, the pioneer of the present-day theme park, even predating Disneyland.

Every day is Christmas in this magical village. Children can talk with Santa and his helpers and visit Santa's home, his workshop, the blacksmith's shop, the glassblower's shop, a church, Mother Hubbard's Cupboard, and several stores.

Santa's famous reindeer are at North Pole, too. In 1955 and 1956, Santa and his reindeer participated in the *Pageant For Peace*, appearing on the front lawn of the White House. The reindeer at North Pole today are direct descendants of the herd flown there in 1953 from Golovan, Alaska. Kept at a ranch in Jay, they are one of the very few herds of reindeer in captivity today.

North Pole has its own U.S. Post Office and zip code, 12946. Visitors bring or send mail to Santa's post office to obtain his unique postmark from the base of Esther Mountain.

By 1960, millions of people had visited Santa Claus, skied the slopes, driven up the highway, or hiked the trails on Esther Mountain. Most, however, still did not know the mountain's name, its folklore, or its natural history. The mountain's natural history began to be appreciated in 1961 when the old Marble Mountain ski lodge became a mecca for scientists, instead of skiers.

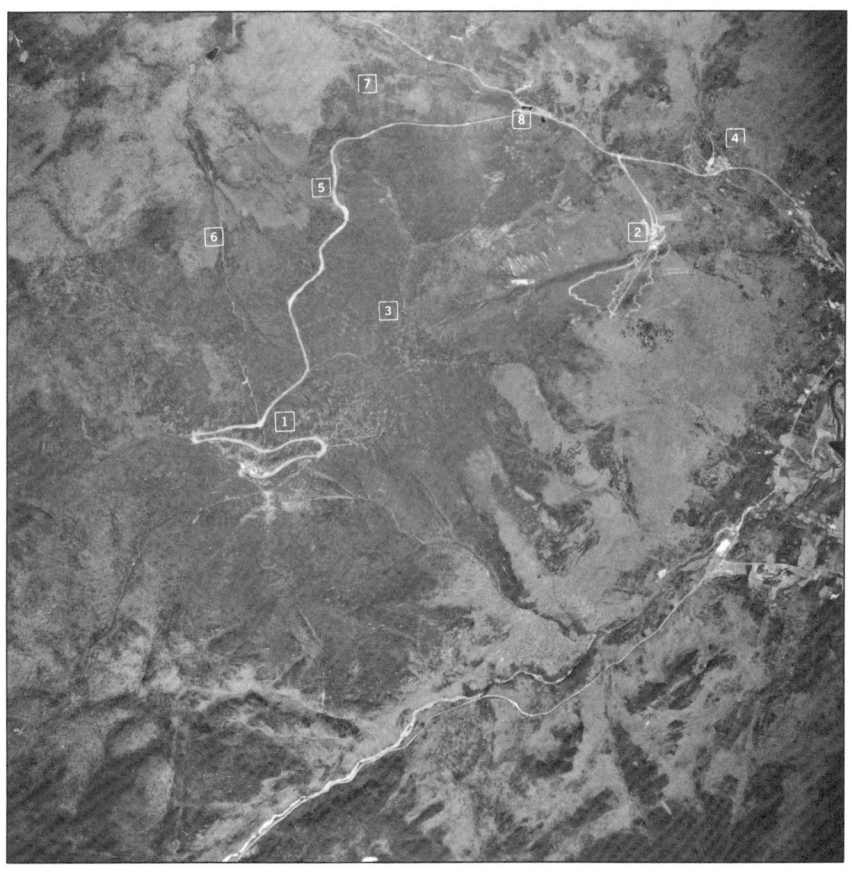

Aerial view, 1952: Whiteface Highway (1), Marble Mountain Ski Center (2), ski trails on Esther Mountain (3), Santa's Workshop (4), Esther Brook (5), French's Brook (6), Schwartz Trail (7), and the gatehouse (8). USGS

DR. EDWIN H. KETCHLEDGE—EDUCATOR

ONCE NEW YORK STATE purchased Esther Mountain from the J. & J. Rogers Company in 1921, the scars of lumbering healed and second-growth forests reclaimed the mountain slopes. The new forests faced new challenges. Automobiles and industrial factories spewed pollutants into the air. Hikers, intent on "peakbagging," caused soil erosion and plant destruction as they tromped up the mountain. And, of course, the forces of wind and cold continued. Both natural and human disturbances kept changing the mountain.

Finally, in the 1950s, attention was focused on the impact of these changes. Esther Mountain began to be viewed, not as a place to be conquered in your car, on your skis, or with your hiking boots but, as a natural museum and living laboratory. In a proposal for a scientific research facility at Whiteface Mountain, Dr. Vincent J. Schaefer is quoted as saying, "It is my considered judgment that there are few better places in the northeastern United States, or even the entire United States, for inaugurating and carrying out the type of educational and research program described in this Memorandum."[1] The report proposed studies on Adirondack thunderstorms, rime ice composition, aurora borealis emissions, cloud seeding, and numerous other subjects to help scientists understand the weather cycle.

In 1961, the State University of New York at Albany established the Atmospheric Sciences Research Center (ASRC), headed by Dr. Schaefer. The ASRC found its home at the old Marble Mountain ski lodge, renamed the Whiteface Mountain Field Station. Dr. Schaefer recalls, "My initial staff consisted of Bernie Vonnegut [Kurt's brother], Ray Falconer [meteorologist], Duncan Blanchard, Austin Hogan, Jim Jiusto, and Dick Orville. As my plans developed, they centered on field and laboratory studies of atmospheric particulates and gaseous reactions in the atmosphere."[2]

Now scientists and environmentalists from around the world perform their research at Whiteface and Esther mountains. They monitor Adirondack weather patterns for national record keeping. From the new three-story observatory on the summit of Whiteface, they analyze the tops of clouds. Using cloud collection equipment on the northwest slopes of Esther Mountain, they analyze the bottoms of clouds. They observe the interactions of clouds and trees and soil. Their studies on atmospheric chemistry and nutrient cycling are crucial to understanding issues such as global warming and acid rain.

The study area on Esther Mountain has three unique aspects. First, ASRC studies conducted in the early 1960s provide statistical data for a long-term study of the Esther Brook watershed. These long-term studies of cloud chemistry are crucial for comparison to current data. There is only one other long-term study area in the entire Northeast.

Second, Whiteface Memorial Highway provides easy, fast, year-round access to the study areas on the side of Esther and the top of Whiteface.

Third, the western and northern slopes of Esther Mountain above 2,700 feet were never clear-cut or burned. Small stands of virgin spruce and fir grow along Whiteface Highway.

Dr. Edwin H. Ketchledge, a Distinguished Teaching Professor Emeritus at S.U.N.Y., College of Environmental Science and Forestry at Syracuse, has been involved with the study of two phenomena on Esther Mountain—the decline of the red spruce and fir waves. Besides teaching and conducting scientific studies, Dr. Ketchledge has been active in educating the public about these changes in the forest.

Dr. Ketchledge has observed that over sixty percent of the mature red spruce growing between 2,500 and 4,000 feet in elevation have been in various stages of decline for over a decade now. Scientists continue to document the details of this decline.

The Esther Brook drainage basin was one of eighteen Field Research Sites across the United States, Canada, and Norway participating in the Integrated Forest Study. The study on atmospheric deposition and forest nutrient cycling states:

> The study site (WF) was located in a narrow west-northwest-trending drainage basin on the flank of Esther Mountain (summit elevation, 1292 m), the eastern peak of the Whiteface massif...The IFS nutrient cycling activities took place between 970 and 1100 m elevation on a north-facing slope of the drainage basin. Airflow at the site was dominated by westerly and northwesterly upslope winds...the study area has not been disturbed by fire or logging in recent history, and can be considered, in general, mature and overmature forest.[3]

The study included experiments such as enclosing declining branches in plastic chambers through which filtered air is passed; determining the concentration, duration, and frequency of the atmospheric pollutants; and comparing the response of seedlings growing naturally with seedlings sheltered from the rain but given pollutant-free water.

The study found that the mortality of red spruce was due in part to natural stresses. Red spruce is very sensitive to both moisture and temperature extremes. Also, spruces keep their leaves for eight years or more, so it takes them longer to recover from winter ice damage, insect attacks, drought, and wind stress. They are susceptible to winter damage because they are the last tree to go hardy in the fall.

Severe winter injury spurred the spruce mortality in the late 1950s through mid-1960s. Winter injury in the 1970s and 1980s sustained the decline. The study concluded, "At current levels, airborne chemicals, especially acid mist, appear to be an important factor in reducing the winter hardiness of red spruce."[4]

Elevation seems to be another factor; red spruce die-back is most prevalent at higher elevations. A study by Battles, Johnson, Siccama, Friedland, and Miller states:

> One explanation for the greater mortality of red spruce at elevations greater than or equal to 1000 m could be that spruce is near the upper extent of its physiological limits and thus is more likely to die at higher elevations than its associates. However, 1000 to 1200 m in elevation is well within red spruce's current and historical range.

The study continues:

> As yet, there is no widely accepted explanation for this elevation effect. LeBlanc (1990) interpreted the greater decline of exposed red spruce as a possible indication of the role of atmospheric stress. Cloud base at Whiteface Mountain is often near or at 1000 m. Consequently, both cloud liquid water content and cloud immersion frequency are subject to large annual variations at approximately 1000 m elevation.[5]

The long-term studies of cloud chemistry by the ASRC show high levels of pollutants at the bottom layer of clouds at 1000 m, the elevation of the Esther Brook study area.

As Dr. Ketchledge explains, "Until we have evaluated *both* the background environmental stresses that may have predisposed this climatically sensitive species to the modern decline, *and* the multi-faceted impacts of atmospheric pollution, we cannot identify the mix of causes or recommend corrective measures to reduce them. . .There are no quick answers to such complex dilemmas."[6]

Today, through continued research, we have more answers about which chemicals are involved and how they interfere with winter hardiness. Dr. Ketchledge explains that nitrogen from atmospheric deposition acts as a

Opposite:
Above: Fir waves on Esther Mountain. Photo by Edwin H. Ketchledge.
Below, left: Research equipment on the slopes of Esther Mountain with declining red spruce in the background. Photo by William L. Weber III.
Below, right: Dr. Ketchledge leading a workshop on Whiteface Mountain. Photo by Nancie Battaglia.

fertilizer which stimulates growth late in the fall season and delays the frost readiness of the tree. Since red spruce is late to go hardy in the fall, this slight delay in frost readiness makes the tree most vulnerable to early winter cold periods.

Scientists do not fully understand why red spruce are decling, but they know it is changing the forest's composition. The immediate effect in the Esther Brook area is an increase in balsam fir. Battles, *et al.* explain that "a compositional shift toward more fir has wide-ranging implications for vegetation dynamics. For example, greater dominance of fir would lead to more rapid canopy turnover, shorter stature forests, and perhaps a greater susceptibility to epidemics."[7]

Another study focuses on the crescent-shaped bands of bare, dying fir trunks present on the upper slopes of Esther Mountain. The gray strips are not the results of pollution, but of natural forest death and regeneration. "This process of cyclic renewal has probably been going on for as long as fir has occupied these mountaintops, maintaining the subalpine forests. . .in much the same state since shortly after the last ice age," explains Peter J. Marchand in his article, "Waves in the Forest." This phenomenon, known as fir waves, is found only on mountains in Japan and the northeastern corner of North America. "The Japanese call it, unpretentiously, 'the mountain with dead tree strips,' " notes Marchand.[8]

A wave starts when a few firs reach maturity, undergo stress, and die, leaving an opening in the tree canopy. The trees exposed along the uphill side are now vulnerable to ice, sun, and winds as high as 121 miles per hour. The trees lose foliage, stop making wood, and suffer root damage. Slowly, they fall and die. Their gray trunks designate the upper edge of the wave. The next uphill row of trees is now exposed to the wind and other stresses. In time, they will begin to deteriorate.

Meanwhile, the downhill side of the opening receives more sunlight and gathers nutrients from the decaying trees. New seedlings quickly establish themselves. Before long, the new growth advances uphill behind the dead gray trunks.

"The term *waves* comes from the double fact that these conspicuous openings do resemble a series of ocean waves breaking on a shoreline *and* are in truth themselves advancing slowly upward a few feet a year under the constant pressure of strong westerly winds," remarks Dr. Ketchledge.[9]

Fir waves are a distinctive feature of the Esther Mountain ridge. "Standing on Whiteface and looking to Esther, we see five such lines of waves seem to be advancing upward. All are indicative of a natural process of even-aged balsam fir regeneration. . ." explained Dr. Ketchledge in 1991.[10] Today, he sits in his parlor looking out at Esther and sees the gaps widening and, in some cases, joining together into bigger gaps. "It's just part of a natural process," he confirms.

Ed Ketchledge also observed the human impact on the mountain. He was instrumental in starting a movement to prevent hikers from "loving the mountains to death." In *The Adirondack Reader*, Paul Jamieson noted, "In the 1960s and 70s the erosion of mountain trails and summit vegetation and 'herd paths' on the trailless peaks pricked the conscience of the Forty-Sixers and others and led to a preservation movement which may possibly qualify as a sixth period in Adirondack mountaineering and which might be called the Edwin Ketchledge period after its prime mover."[11]

As president of the Adirondack Forty-Sixers in 1976, Ed Ketchledge suggested the club assist with trail maintenance to "give something back to the mountains." He also began a program to protect and restore the alpine summits. On several peaks, summit stewards greet hikers and educate them about the fragile alpine tundra at their feet. Ketchledge also leads workshops on alpine vegetation, organizes revegetation work parties, and publishes articles on forest ecology and protection for the Adirondack Mountain Club, the Adirondack Forty-Sixers, and the Adirondack Nature Conservancy. He writes:

> ...With the disappearance of the virgin wilderness came appreciation for what we had lost, and an emerging consensus to let natural processes reclaim as much of the unoccupied landscape as political reality would allow. The New York State Constitution guarantees that process. Meanwhile, we as citizens enjoying the natural forest resources and landscape beauty have our personal and private responsibility to abet those natural recovery processes; to pursue our recreational activities without abusing the environment and biota; to encourage responsible woodsmanship and low-impact recreation whenever we traverse the landscape; and to preserve the natural beauty and diversity of our Adirondack homeland we love and enjoy. Our own activities in the grand scene must be compatible with the natural processes of restoration characteristic of the landscape as first inherited by our forefathers arriving on these mountain shores so long ago.[12]

Esther Mountain is one of the few high peaks with a spruce and fir forest standing as it was over 300 years ago. The virgin forest in Esther Brook basin escaped the Goodspeed farmers, the hikers of French's Trail, the J. & J. Rogers Company lumbermen, the forest fires, the Marble Mountain skiers, and the Whiteface Highway builders. Studies of Esther Mountain can help scientists understand the long-term processes of the forests and the effects of air pollution on the Adirondacks and the world.

A GUIDED TOUR

WHEN YOU ARE LURED to Esther Mountain be forewarned—Esther Mountain is difficult to find. To fully appreciate Esther Mountain requires travel. Ideally, it requires an oxen-pulled wagon or a stagecoach, although a motorcar will suffice.

The easiest place to begin your tour is the village of Lake Placid. From the shore of Mirror Lake, look up at the pyramid-shaped Whiteface Mountain with its gleaming birthmarks. The 4,867 foot Whiteface completely hides the slightly smaller Esther.

Head east out of Lake Placid toward Wilmington on Route 86. When you reach the stop sign in Wilmington, turn right. Stop near the stone bridge. This is the best view in town. From here, Marble, Lookout, Whiteface, and Esther mountains are visible. To the far right you can see part of White Brook Cirque. If you have time, continue out of town toward Jay for more views.

Turn around and head back on Route 86 to the stop sign. Continue straight up the Whiteface Memorial Highway along the side of Esther Mountain. On your left is the start of a hiking trail to Whiteface. At 1.6 miles is the North Pole and Santa's Workshop.

Farther up the road, a sign on the left indicates the home of the Atmospheric Sciences Research Center. Turn left and drive down to the wooden building. Notice the huge logs from the blowdown of 1950. Imagine what it must have been like to ski here fifty years ago.

Drive back to the Whiteface Highway, turn left, and continue up the mountain. At the Y in the road, follow the sign left to "White Face Mt." Continue through the gatehouse and up the Whiteface Mountain Veterans Memorial Highway. As you drive, notice the gentle grade, the stone support walls, and the rocks with scars from drilling or blasting.

About 1.6 miles from the gatehouse, the road crosses Esther Brook. You can pull off on the right. Notice the stands of old growth spruce and fir. From your car you can see the collection tower and other scientific equipment positioned on the slopes of the mountain. This is the scientific study area, which is strictly *OFF LIMITS* to visitors.

A half mile up the road is another pulloff. This is a good spot from which to view the mountain forest. Walk back to where French's Brook passes under the highway. Imagine a wagon hauling tourists up French's valley. A blue mark on a rock .4 miles up the road was probably meant to show the route of French's Trail up the mountain.

Look at the trees in French's valley; the mountain birch and hardwoods thrive. On the mountainside, the red spruce dominate the canopy. High up on Esther Mountain, fir waves span across the slopes. *Krummholz* covers the summit.

The best place to see Esther Mountain is from the top of Whiteface Mountain. Continue to the castle at the top of Whiteface. Walk up the short nature trail along the rocky ridge. At the summit, avoid the crowd and walk to the left (east) side of the silo where you can catch a fantastic view of Esther and escape from the prevailing westerly wind.

From Whiteface, look along the three-mile ridge to Esther's summit. Below Esther lies the small pond on French's Brook, the fertile fields of St. Armand, the Whiteface Highway, the Saranac River, and the Ausable River.

From the other side of the silo you can follow the view from Lake Placid through the High Falls Gorge, past Whiteface Ski Center and Wilmington, and up to the other high peaks.

Return to your car via the twenty-seven-story elevator and granite tunnel. Head down the mountain. After you pass through the gatehouse, stop at the holding pond on your right. About 1895, this pond was dammed with rocks cut from the quarry across the road. The dam released water into the log trough that sent pulp wood down to the Ausable River. You can still see the dam and the overgrown trough path.

About half a mile down Red Brook and thirty years back in time, beehive-shaped coal kilns stood beside the brook. The J. & J. Rogers Company operated three charcoal kilns and owned some dwellings at this site.

The Friends of Whiteface hope to develop a "Trail of History" on the lower slopes of Whiteface and Esther mountains. The trail will take you through the sites of the charcoal kilns, lumber camps, log flume, holding pond, and rock quarry.

After you leave the pond, turn left at the Y and continue on St. Armand Road toward Franklin Falls and Bloomingdale. Half a mile down the hill, a sign reading "Cooper Kiln Pond, 2.7 miles" marks a trail off to the right. This old logging road led to Little Montreal lumber village and through the woods to the J. & J. Rogers Company charcoal kilns near Cooper Kiln (Morgan) Pond. The gravity railroad led from this trail to the West Kilns on Black Brook (Plank) Road.

Just across the road is the start of the Schwartz Trail. It was used as a lumber road by J. & J. Rogers Company and was part of the 1932 Olympic Cross-Country Ski Trail.

Continue down the mountain one mile until you reach the sign "Town of St. Armand" and a pulloff on the right. Somewhere near this town boundary stood the house of Thomas Combs. This is Lot #381.

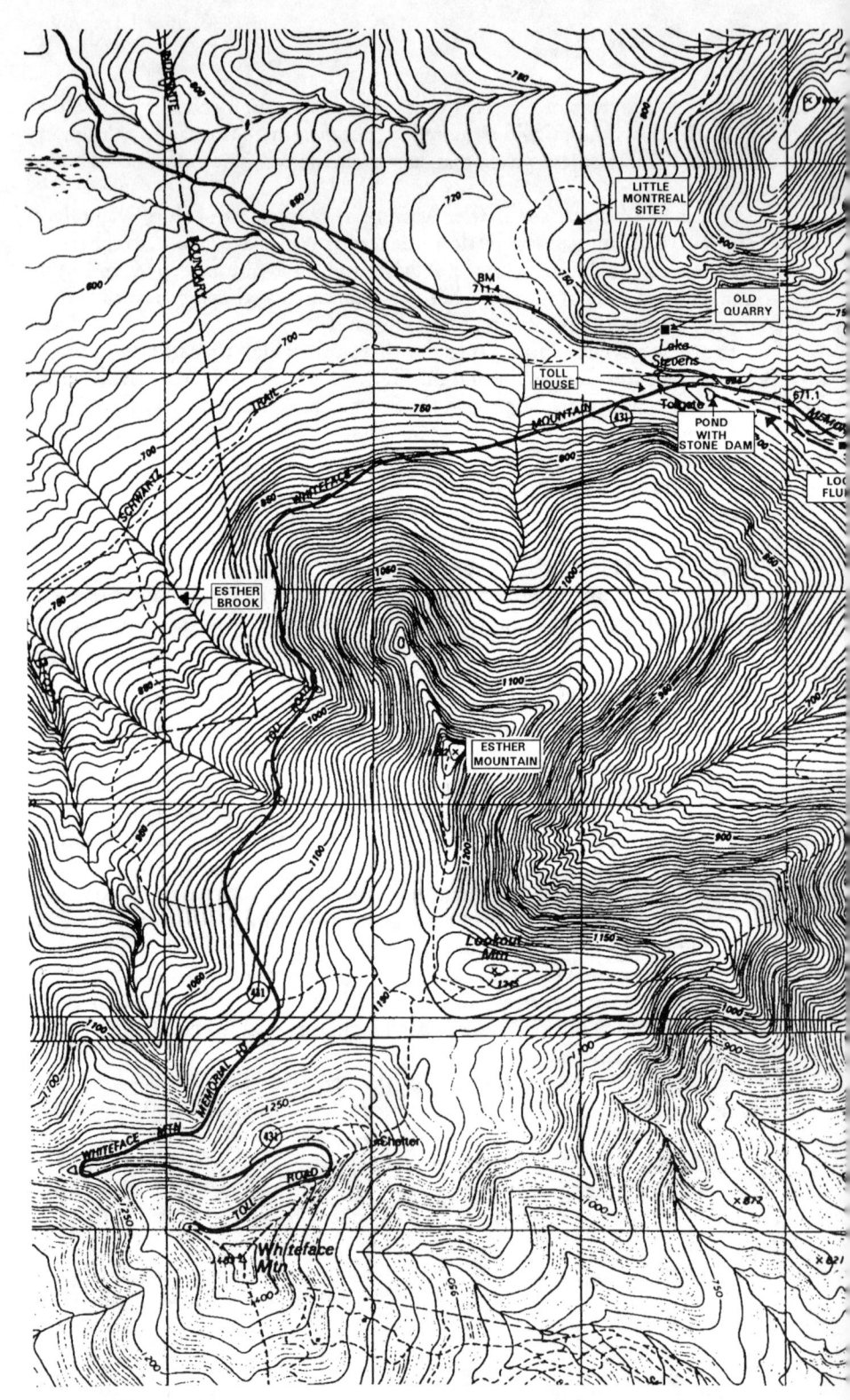

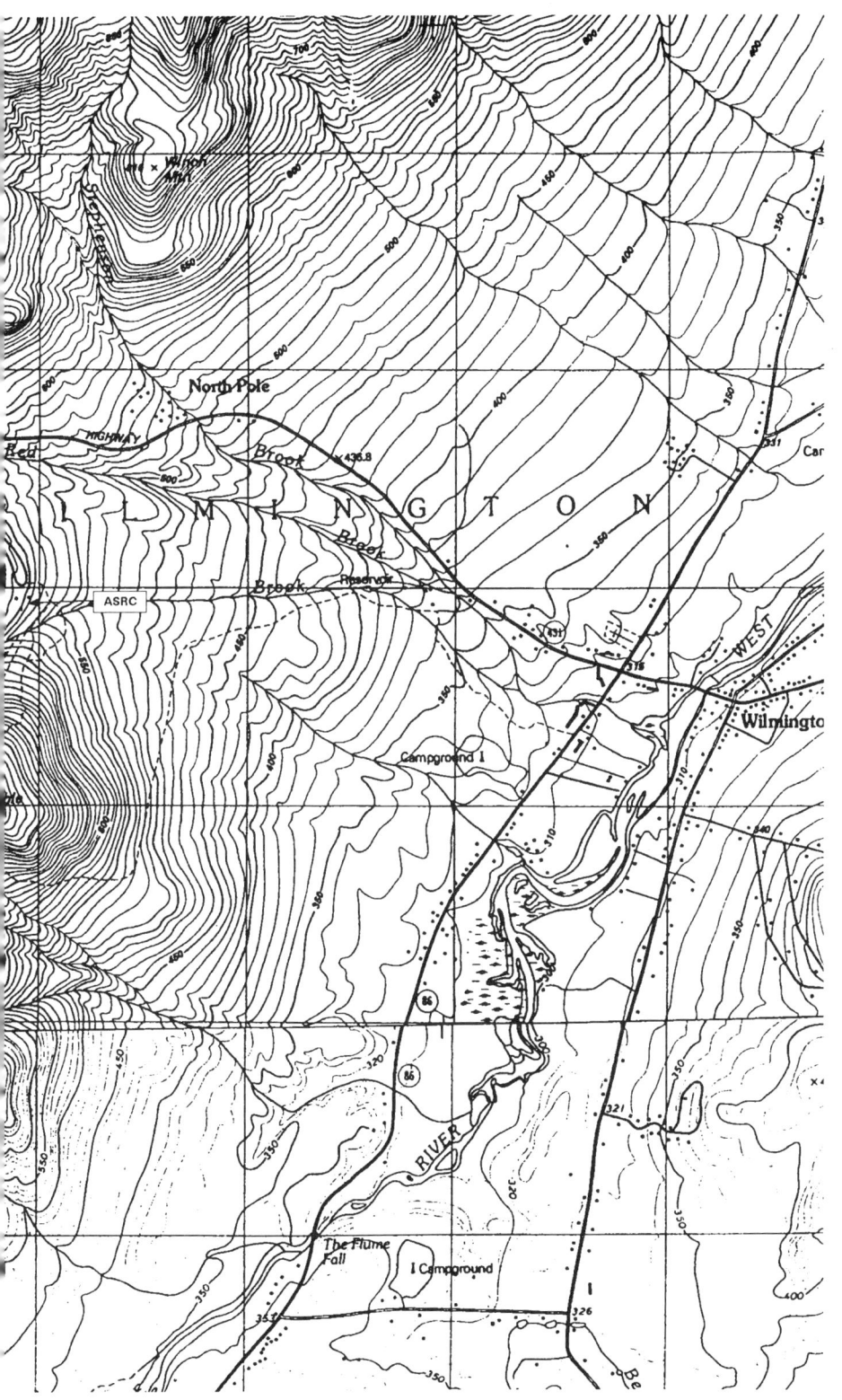

USGS map enhancements by Brendan Blake.

Farther down the mountain, you can find what is left of the Goodspeed farm, French's settlement, Plank Road, and Franklin Falls. About two miles down the road, there is a deadend road on the left known as John Simond's Road. Head down this dirt road to the Goodspeed Cemetery. Farther down the road you can drive past Elias Goodspeed's house and the pine plantation.

Back on the main road to Franklin Falls, you pass Union Cemetery. Up on this hill are the graves of the pioneers of this area, including Wallace Goodspeed and Luman, Clarissa, and Samuel French.

Continue west for two miles until you cross Franklin Falls Reservoir. There is no village or grand hotel here, so turn around and cross back over the bridge. Drive 1.6 miles and turn left on Plank Road. About 1.4 miles down the road is Rosmond Lane on the right leading back to St. Armand. A roadsign at the intersection reads "Plank Road." This intersection was the settlement of French's, now called Forestdale.

As you continue straight on Plank Road toward Black Brook, there are several magnificent views of Esther and Whiteface mountains with Esther in the foreground and Whiteface behind her. This is the area of West Kilns, where the gravity railroad ended.

To return to Wilmington, turn around and go back to French's. Turn left, follow the road to the end, and turn left onto the St. Armand Road. Back at Wilmington, you may want to take a hike.

Before you step into the woods, remember that Esther Mountain is a trailless peak. Although there is a well-trodden herd path on Esther, it is not marked or maintained. Make sure you have the skills and equipment required to climb a trailless mountain. *Guide to Adirondack Trails: High Peaks Region*, edited by Tony Goodwin and published by the Adirondack Mountain Club, is an excellent source for information on hiking preparedness and the trails of the area.

Three trails lead to the herd path up Esther Mountain. The most popular starts at the Wilmington Reservoir. Another trail starts at the Atmospheric Sciences Research Center. These two trails join and head up the south rim of White Brook drainage bowl and then to the top of Lookout Mountain. The herd path to the summit of Esther Mountain leads off to the right. For a shorter hike, you could drive to the top of Whiteface and hike down the Wilmington trail to the herd path turnoff. Of course, this hike would not qualify as a Forty-Sixer climb.

When you reach the summit of Esther Mountain, imagine Esther Combs standing there 156 years ago looking up at the mighty Whiteface. Imagine Russell French there 120 years ago. Imagine Wallace Goodspeed there 95 years ago, Grace Hudowalski 56 years ago, and Ed Ketchledge last year. Imagine who will be standing there 50 years from now.

CONCLUSION

ESTHER MOUNTAIN has been dug, cut, blasted, burned, stripped, paved, and ignored. It has lost its pristine wilderness character but it still offers unique opportunities for tourists, scientists, and hikers.

Tourists can drive on the northernmost Adirondack high peak, the only peak named for a woman. They can view the mountain's birthmarks and forest regrowth, its cirque and *Krummholz*, broomsticks and boulders. They can explore the scattered traces of man's past interaction with the mountain and imagine the farm fields, log flumes, plank roads, and charcoal kilns.

Scientists can study the fir waves and the decline of red spruce in the old forest. They investigate interactions of clouds and trees and soil. Their findings are crucial to understanding forestry issues affecting the Adirondacks and the world.

Hikers can climb Esther Mountain for the "sheer joy of climbing." They climb to enjoy the view, the forest, and the wildlife. In just two hours they can hike from Whiteface to Esther and enjoy the wilderness experience Esther Combs did in 1839.

Tourists, scientists, hikers—folk like Russell French, Grace Hudowalski, Russ Carson, and Ed Ketchledge—have been lured to the high peak on the shoulder of Whiteface. They have discovered Esther's special history, mystery, and majesty.

Esther is the Matriarch of the Adirondack High Peaks.

Esther Mountain summit canister.
Photo by the author.

NOTES

Birthmarks

1. Howard W. and Elizabeth B. Jaffe, *Geology of the Adirondack High Peaks Region, A Hiker's Guide* (Lake George, NY: The Adirondack Mountain Club, Inc., 1986), 1.
2. Laura and Guy Waterman, *Forest and Crag: A History of Hiking, Trail Blazing, and Adventure in the Northeast Mountains* (Boston: Appalachian Mountain Club, 1989), 121.
3. Linda Lumsden, "Weather Watch at Whiteface," *Adirondack Daily Enterprise Weekender* (April 19, 1985), 3.
4. Donald Culross Peattie, *A Natural History of Trees of Eastern and Central North America* (Boston: Houghton Mifflin Company, 1950), 51.

Early Settlers

1. W. C. Redfield, "Some Account of Two Visits to the Mountains in Essex County, New York, in the Years 1836 and 1837; With a Sketch of the Northern Sources of the Hudson," *The Family Magazine* (from *The American Journal of Science and Arts*) 5 (1838), 347-8.
2. Horatio Gates Spafford, *A Gazetteer of the State of New-York* (Albany, NY: H. C. Southwick, 1813), 215.
3. Ibid.
4. Russell M. L. Carson, *Peaks and People of the Adirondacks* (1927; reprint, with a preface by George Marshall, introduction by Philip G. Terrie, Jr., and map by Jerome S. Kates, Glens Falls, NY: The Adirondack Mountain Club, 1973), 18.
5. Ebenezer Emmons, *Geology of New-York. Part II Comprising the Survey of the Second Geological District.* (Albany, NY: 1842), 220.
6. *The Opening of the Adirondacks* (New York: Hurd and Houghton, 1865), 27.
7. Adeline F. Jacques, *Echoes from Whiteface Mountain: A Brief History of Wilmington, New York* (Published by author, 1980), 2.
8. *200 Years of Methodism 1784-1984, 150 Years of the Whiteface Community United Methodist Church, Wilmington, New York 1834-1984* (1984).
9. S. R. Stoddard, *The Adirondacks: Illustrated* (1874; reprint, Glens Falls, NY: Coneco Laser Graphics, Inc., 1983), 55.
10. Weston Arthur Goodspeed, *History of the Goodspeed Family, Volume I* (Chicago: W.A. Goodspeed, 1907), 19 and 33.
11. Ibid., 211.
12. H. P. Smith, ed., *The History of Essex County, With Illustrations and Biographical Sketches of Some of its Prominent Men and Pioneers* (Syracuse, NY: D. Mason & Co., 1885), 651.
13. Goodspeed, *History of Goodspeed Family*, 212.
14. National Archives, Veterans Records for Wallace Goodspeed, Company D, 17th Regiment Vermont Infantry.

Esther Combs--First Climber

1 Carson, *Peaks and People*, 96-97.
2 Penny Wiktorek, "Legends of the Adirondacks," in *Of the Summits, of the Forests*, ed. Tim Tefft (Morrisonville, NY: Adirondack Forty-Sixers, 1991), 233-5. Reprinted, with permission of Adirondack Forty-Sixers.
3 J. H. French, *Map of Essex County New York* (Philadelphia: W. O. Shearer & E. A. Balch, 1858).
4 Charles Beede to Carson, April 1924?, Russell Carson Papers, Adirondack Museum Library.
5 Vital Records of Gill, Mass. to the year 1850 by New England Historical Genealogical Society. The Church of Jesus Christ of Latter-day Saints, Film 0823731, Item 3.
6 Essex County Deed Record, Book RR, 327-8.
7 Census for State of New York, County of Essex, Town of St. Armand, Agricultural Statistics, 1855.
8 Real and Personal Estate Assessment Roll for State of New York, County of Essex, Town of St. Armand, 1855.
9 Coleman, age 16, is listed in the 1850 census. Alva C., age 21, is listed in the 1855 census. Alva C. and Alvah C. are listed in two deeds. I conclude that these refer to the same person, named Alvah Coleman Combs.
10 Julia, age 8, is listed in the 1850 census. Julia A., age 18, is listed in the 1860 census. Ann, age 15, is listed only in the 1855 census (and Julia is not). I conclude that Ann's age in the 1855 census was mistaken and that Julia and Ann refer to the same person, Julia Ann Combs.
11 James Goodwin, letter to author, August 2, 1994.
12 Essex County Deed Record, Book 53, 106.

Russell French--First Trail Blazer

1 John J. Duquette, "Franklin Falls," *Adirondack Daily Enterprise*, (April 13, 1987), 10.
2 Hamilton Child, *History of Clinton and Franklin County* (Philadelphia: J. W. Lewis & Co., 1880), 376.
3 "Life Story of James M. Wolfe, Civil War Veteran," (1931), 1.
4 Map of Franklin County New York (Philadelphia: Taintor, Dawson, and Co., 1858).
5 S. R. Stoddard, *The Adirondacks: Illustrated* (Glens Falls, NY: the author, 1879), 62.
6 E. R. Wallace, *Descriptive Guide to the Adirondacks*. (Syracuse, NY: the author, 1880), Addenda.
7 *Atlas of Franklin County, New York* (Philadelphia: D. G. Beers and Co., 1876).
8 Waterman, *Forest and Crag*, 65.
9 Alfred Billings Street, *The Indian Pass* (1869; reprint, Harrison, NY: Harbor Hill Books, 1975), 126.
10 G. T. S., "Visit to White Face," *The Elizabethtown Post and Gazette* (August 13, 1859), 1.
11 El Hayes, "The Pony Trail to Whiteface," *Lake Placid News* (June 22, 1928).
12 "A Pilgrimage to John Brown's Mountain," *The Knickerbocker or New-York Monthly Magazine* 59 (1862), 236-7.
13 Wallace, *Descriptive Guide to Adirondacks*, addenda.
14 Stoddard, *The Adirondacks: Illustrated* (1882), 61, 217.
15 James Goodwin, letter to author, July 27, 1993.

16 Verplanck Colvin, *Topographical Survey: Adirondack Region of New York, Third to Seventh Report 1874-1879*, 213.
17 Wallace, *Descriptive Guide to Adirondacks* (1894), 274.
18 Letha Ryder, "Whiteface--Then and Now," *Cloudsplitter* 6, no. 8 (November 1943), 3.
19 Robert Marshall, *The High Peaks of the Adirondacks* (Albany, NY: The Adirondack Mountain Club, Inc., 1922), 14.
20 James Goodwin, letter to author, September 14, 1994.

J. & J. Rogers Company--Landowners and Loggers

1 Essex County Deed Record, Book LL, 237-8.
2 Child, *History of Clinton and Franklin County*, 253.
3 Essex County Deed Record, Book 53, 131-2.
4 Helen E. Tyler, *Mountain Memories: Folk Tales of the Adirondacks*. (Privately published, 1974), 56-7.
5 Ibid., 64-6.
6 W. O. Gray, *New Topographical Atlas of Essex County, New York* (Philadelphia: Walker, Jewett & Miller, 1876).
7 Although Tyler refers to the "northwest side of Whiteface Mountain" several times, I believe Little Montreal was located on the northeast side. She refers to the toll gate, which is on the northeast side. The 1876 map, an old-timer's recollections, and the description of the railroad all point to the location just northeast of the toll gate.
8 Essex County Deed Record, Book 53, 338.
9 Child, *History of Clinton and Franklin County*, 256.
10 "Noted Men and Women of the Champlain Valley and the Adirondacks," unsourced scrapbook, Rogers Vertical File, Adirondack Museum Library.
11 Real and Personal Estate Assessment Roll for State of New York, County of Essex, Town of Wilmington, 1886.
12 Elsa C. Voelcker, *An Industrial History of Au Sable Forks New York* (Rochester, NY: E.C.V. at the Visual Studies Workshop, 1976).
13 Ibid.
14 William F. Fox, *History of the Lumber Industry in the State of New York* (1901; reprint, Harrison, New York: Harbor Hill Books, 1976), 77.
15 Essex County Deed Record, Book 166, 102.

Russell Carson--First Historian

1 Marshall, *The High Peaks of the Adirondacks*, 3.
2 Ibid., 30.
3 Carson to Thomas C. Stowell, January 6, 1924, Russell Carson Papers.
4 Scott Brown to Carson, January 23, 1923, Russell Carson Papers.
5 M. J. Trumbull to Carson, February 4, 1923, Russell Carson Papers.
6 Scott Brown to Carson, April 4, 1923, Russell Carson Papers.
7 Robert Marshall to Carson, May 16, 1923, Russell Carson Papers.
8 Carson to Robert Marshall, May 26, 1923, Russell Carson Papers.
9 Carson to Scott Brown, November 11, 1923, Russell Carson Papers.
10 Ibid.
11 Charles Beede to Carson, April 1924?, Russell Carson Papers.

12 Carson to Robert Marshall, April 5, 1926, Russell Carson Papers.
13 Robert Marshall to Carson, December 6, 1924, Russell Carson Papers.
14 Alfred L. Donaldson, *A History of the Adirondacks, Volume I* (1921; reprint, with a new introduction by John J. Duquette, Fleischmanns, NY: Purple Mountain Press, Ltd., 1992), 268-70.

Grace Hudowalski--First Steward

1 Grace L. Hudowalski, "Esther," *The Cloudsplitter* (April 1939), 4.
2 Grace L. Hudowalski and C. Howard Nash, "21 Trailless Peaks," *The Adirondack Mountain Club Yearbook* (January 1939), 24.
3 Hudowalski, "Esther," 5.
4 *Epworth Embers* was a young people's magazine written and published by the Grace Methodist Church in Troy.
5 Grace L. Hudowalski, Personal Notes, Esther Centennial Ceremony, 1939.
6 "Mt. Esther Centennial," *The August Reporter* (Albany Chapter, The Adirondack Mountain Club, 1939?).

New Developments

1 George Horace Lorimer, "Nibbling," *The Saturday Evening Post* 7 (January 1928), 32.
2 Louis Marshall, "Opposes White Face Road," *New York Times*, letter to editor dated November 3, 1927.
3 Russell Carson, "Trail Builder Gives Views Opposing Road Up Mount Whiteface," *The Adirondack Enterprise* (February 16, 1927), 2.
4 Theodore Marvin, "Whiteface Mountain Highway," *The Explosives Engineer* 12 (October 1934), 286.
5 Ibid., 285.
6 Red Buck, "Life on the Summit," *Adirondack Life* (Winter 1973), 14-15.
7 S. M. Serebreny, "Whiteface Mountain Meteorological Observatory," *Mount Washington Observatory News Bulletin* (February 1938), 2.
8 James Goodwin, letter to author, August 2, 1994.
9 "$250,000," *The New Yorker* 17, no. 47 (November 15, 1941), 18.
10 James Goodwin, letter to author, August 2, 1994.
11 "Northeast, Whiteface/Placid: High and Mighty," *Snow Country* (September 1994), 178.

Dr. Edwin H. Ketchledge--Educator

1 Scientific Advisory Committee to the Whiteface Mountain Authority, *The Scientific Utilization of Whiteface Mountain* (Wilmington, NY: 1958).
2 Vincent J. Schaefer, "How to Have Fun," in *ASRC Report 1988-1991: 30th Anniversary* (Albany, NY: University at Albany, State University of New York, 1992), 8.
3 Dale W. Johnson and Steven E. Lindberg, eds., *Ecological Studies Volume 91: Atmospheric Deposition and Forest Nutrient Cycling-A Synthesis of the Integrated Forest Study* (New York: Springer-Verlag, 1992), 13-14.
4 Ibid., 524.
5 John J. Battles et al., "Red Spruce Death: Effects on Forest Composition and Structure on Whiteface Mountain, New York," *Bulletin of the Torrey Botanical Club* 119, no. 4 (1992), 425-8.

6 Edwin H. Ketchledge, "Red Spruce Decline in the Adirondack High Country," *Adirondac* (February/March 1988), 15-16.
7 Battles, "Red Spruce Death," 429.
8 Peter J. Marchand, "Waves in the Forest," *Natural History* 104, No. 2 (February 1995), 26 and 32.
9 Edwin H. Ketchledge, "Fir Waves," *Adirondac* (June 1988), 20.
10 Edwin H. Ketchledge, "Summits and Forests of the Adirondack High Country," in *Of the Summits, of the Forests*, 187.
11 Paul Jamieson, *The Adirondack Reader* (Glens Falls, NY: The Adirondack Mountain Club, Inc., 1982), 389 n.
12 Edwin H. Ketchledge, "Welcome to Whiteface Mountain," Notes from Adirondack Nature Conservancy Workshop, 2.

PURPLE MOUNTAIN PRESS is a publishing company committed to producing the best original books of regional interest as well as bringing back into print significant older works. Adirondack titles include:

A HISTORY OF THE ADIRONDACKS
by Alfred L. Donaldson

Donaldson's *History* is recognized as the major work about the entire region and, as such, has remained unsurpassed since its first publication in 1921. This is an unabridged reprint with a biographical sketch of Donaldson by John Duquette.
766 pages in two volumes, illustrated, cloth.

WILDLIFE AND WILDERNESS
A History of Adirondack Mammals
by Philip G. Terrie

A thorough cultural history of man's interaction with fur-bearing and game animals. This book examines the extirpation of the moose, elk, panther, and beaver and the politics, ethics, and ecology that play a part in attempts to reintroduce some of the large mammals to their former ranges.
176 pages, illustrated, paperback.

ON THE ADIRONDACK SURVEY WITH VERPLANCK COLVIN
The Diaries of Percy Reese Morgan
edited with an introduction by Norman J. Van Valkenburgh

Percy Reese Morgan (1878-1961) was a college student when he joined the crew of Verplanck Colvin's famed Adirondack Survey. His diaries provide a candid look at camp life during the summers of 1895 and 1896.
96 pages, illustrated, paperback.

THE INDIAN PASS
Source of the Hudson
by Alfred Billings Street

Wilderness was total when Street set out to find the source of the Hudson on Mount Marcy in 1869. This reprint provides a nostalgic look at mid-19th century Adirondack exploration.
264 pages, paperback.

Available at bookstores or order from the publisher:
PURPLE MOUNTAIN PRESS, LTD.
P.O. Box E3, Fleischmanns, New York 12430, 914-254-4062
A free catalog lists over 300 hard-to-find books about New York State.